Disclaimer and Copyright

Text Copyright © Siim Land 2016

All rights reserved. No part of this guide may be reproduced in any form without permission in writing from the publisher except in the case of brief quotations embodied in critical articles or reviews.

Legal & Disclaimer

The information contained in this book is not designed to replace or take the place of any form of medicine or professional medical advice. The information in this book has been provided for educational and entertainment purposes only.

The information contained in this book has been compiled from sources deemed reliable, and it is accurate to the best of the Author's knowledge;

however, the Author cannot guarantee its accuracy and validity and cannot be held liable for any errors or omissions. Changes are periodically made to this book. You must consult your doctor or get professional medical advice before using any of the suggested remedies, techniques, or information in this book.

Upon using the information contained in this book, you agree to hold harmless the Author from and against any damages, costs, and expenses, including any legal fees potentially resulting from the application of any of the information provided by this guide. This disclaimer applies to any damages or injury caused by the use and application, whether directly or indirectly, of any advice or information presented, whether for breach of contract, tort, negligence, personal injury, criminal intent, or under any other cause of action.

You agree to accept all risks of using the information presented inside this book. You need to consult a professional medical practitioner in order to ensure you are both able and healthy enough to participate in this program.

All rights reserved. No part of this publication may be reproduced, distributed, or transmitted in any form or by any means, including photocopying, recording, or other electronic or mechanical methods, without the prior written permission of the publisher, except in the case of brief quotations embodied in critical reviews and certain other noncommercial uses permitted by copyright law. For permission requests, contact the publisher, at the address below.

http://www.siimland.com.

Cover design by Siim Land.

Table of Contents

Disclaimer and Copyright 1

Table of Contents 4

Introduction The Circle of Life 7

Chapter I Some Keto Fundamentals 13

    Indigenous Ketogenic Societies 18

    Is Ketosis Safe 20

    The Most Relevant Hormones 23

    How to Get into Ketosis 29

        Carbohydrates. 30

        Protein 35

        Fats 38

    How to Know You Are in Ketosis 42

Chapter II Why Do the Ketogenic Diet 47

    Ketosis for Health 50

    Athletes Going Against the Grain (Pun Intended) 51

    Keto Smart 59

Chapter III Return of the Carbohydrate Paradigm Shift 65

    Do You Need Carbs? 71

    All That Work for Nothing? 74

    Keto Adaptation vs Nutritional Ketosis 76

- Chapter IV The Standard Cyclical Ketogenic Diet ... 79
  - The Downside to the Standard Cyclical Ketogenic Diet ... 86
- Chapter V Who Should do the Cyclical Ketogenic Diet ... 89
  - How to Workout on Keto ... 92
- Chapter VI Enter the Keto Cycle ... 95
  - Stage I Adaptation ... 96
  - Stage II Replenish and Supercompensate ... 101
  - Stage III The Cycle Begins ... 107
- Chapter VII Mistakes to Avoid to Not Get Lost in the Eye of the Storm ... 111
  - The Deadly Sins NOT to Do ... 116
- Chapter VIII Keto Cycle Supplementation ... 120
  - Natural Seasoning ... 122
  - Supplements you HAVE to Take ... 126
  - Supplements Empowered ... 128
  - Keto Cycle Supplements ... 133
- Bonus Chapter The Keto Cycle Cookbook ... 135
  - Ketogenic Recipes ... 136
    - The Ultimate Breakfast ... 136
    - Fatty Egg Yolk Coffee ... 138
    - Bone Broth Soup ... 141
    - Meaty Vegetable Roast-Feast ... 144
    - Cauliflower Pizza ... 146
    - Cheesy Tomato Soup ... 149
    - Beef Stroganoff ... 151

- Keto Spaghetti Squash ... 153
- Coconut Milk Ice Cream ... 155
- Keto Pancakes ... 157
- Glycemic Recipes ... 159
    - Homemade French Fries ... 160
    - Chicken Curry ... 162
    - Rice Pudding ... 164
    - Beetroot Potato Salad with Honey ... 166
    - Low Glycemic Stew ... 167
- Conclusion Break the Cycle and Go Beyond ... 170
- KETO CARB CYCLE Meal Plan ... 172
- More Books from the Author ... 173
- Leave a Review on Amazon! ... 176
- About the Author. ... 177
- Reference ... 178

Introduction

The Circle of Life

As a leaf in the thick evergreen rainforest falls to the ground, it instantly enters a cycle of composting. The humidity and bugs begin to immediately break it down into its tiniest of particles. What comes out is food for the parasites and manure for the soil. Upon this death and destruction newborn life will sprout into existence in another form.

Everything in this world is in constant motion. Starting with the Sun, rivers, atmospheric circulation and ending with the movements of animals, our moods and muscle contractions. Even Earth itself is in a cycle of swallowing continents and forging them into new solid rocks. It's happening all around us.

In the world of dieting it's the same. Our body is never under similar conditions as it was the day before. As we get older, bigger, stronger or more physically active, so will our energy demands increase. On the flip side, if we move less, then we don't have to eat as much either.

The only constant is change. It's all a game of balance. Even our metabolism comes into play, as we're tapping between being a fed and a fasted state. At least during the night.

By picking up this book, chances are you've already heard about the ketogenic diet. That's great because it will make the content in here that much easier to understand. If not, don't worry either, we'll cover some of the fundamentals you should know in the first chapter.

Keto Cycle takes the standard ketogenic diet and turns it into the cyclical variation of it. It has been successfully used by athletes, bodybuilders, powerlifters and even obese dieters to lose excess body fat and build muscle.

Low carb eating is not the end-all-be-all, although it's extremely effective and sustainable. For people who train hard it may have some performance decrements because of their high demands. Also, maintaining a standard ketogenic diet requires a lot of attention and effort, which isn't as important on the cyclical approach.

My name is Siim Land and I've been practicing some form of the ketogenic diet for a long time now and have become very fat adapted. Having done a lot of self-experimentations and quantifying I can consider myself quite the expert in the field. I've researched the topic thoroughly and have made some pretty impressive gains as a result of that.

My performance has increased in terms of my physical and cognitive abilities. I've managed to change my biology in a way that reduces hunger, muscle catabolism and fatigue close to zero, even into the negatives. On top of that I'm always energized and if I'm tired, then it usually has to do with a poor night's sleep, not nutrition.

The Keto Cycle helps me to effortlessly maintain a single digit body fat percentage year-round. It's not a diet, because you don't have to obsessively measure your food intake to meet your goals. This plan is structured in a way that everything happens almost automatically. You don't even have to think about it and it's very easy to follow. To be honest, I've never felt or looked better.

The cyclical ketogenic diet is most often used by low carb athletes but it can work for anyone. You can construct your own plan according to your personal condition and preference. This makes it very enjoyable and applicable to any goal.

Whatever the case might be, you will most definitely benefit from reading this.

The Keto cycle can be used to

- Lose body fat and get shredded without depriving your body.
- Build muscle and size while not getting fat.
- Get stronger, faster and more powerful as an athlete.
- Battle diabetes and reverse other medical conditions.
- Improve mental focus and attain Jedi-like concentration.
- Protect yourself against cancer, tumors and coronary heart disease.
- Increase your longevity and insulin sensitivity.
- Become fat adapted and start using fat for fuel.
- Experience mental clarity and feel amazing.
- Have access to abundant energy all of the time.
- Reduce your hunger and lose sugar cravings for good.
- Eat mouthwatering and delicious meals that leave you satiated for longer, including carbs.

As the circle of life and death continues, so does the Keto Cycle. It's a very sustainable way of eating that doesn't neglect any food group entirely. You can even eat some junk if you'd like, although you don't have to. What's best is that you won't get addicted to it and can easily get away with consuming some carbs. All while maintaining your ketogenic pathways.

Let the Keto Cycle begin!

Chapter I

Some Keto Fundamentals

Before we start, we have to get into nutritional ketosis. Otherwise this plan won't work. That's why we'll briefly cover some of the fundamentals of keto. So, here we go. I could even explain it to a child.

There are different fuel sources the body uses. When we're born, we get all of the energy we need from our mother's breast milk, at least that's what we did in the past, which puts us into ketosis. As we grow up, we begin to eat different foods, comprising of the 3 macronutrients: protein, carbs and fat. This primes our body to be using glucose, which is a carbohydrate molecule, and sets it as our primary default fuel source. There's nothing wrong with that, the thing is that in today's society most people have drifted too far away from their aboriginal ketogenic pathways, which causes obesity, diabetes and other ailments. Luckily, there is a way to circumvent that.

The human body is a complex system that can adapt to almost anything. It has found a solution to solving the bioenergetics component of being self-sufficient and resourceful. Ketosis is just that – an irreplaceable part of our biology that creates endogenous (from within) energy.

In a nutshell, ketosis is a metabolic state in which the body has shifted from using glucose as the primary fuel source into supplying its energy demands with ketone bodies.

This happens when the liver glycogen stores are depleted and a substitute is necessary for the brain to maintain its functioning.

Both carbohydrates and fats can be used for the production of energy, but they're different in quality. However, in the presence of both, the body will always prefer carbs because sugar can be easily accessed and quickly absorbed. To get the most out of the ketones and fatty acids, there needs to be a period of keto-adaptation. The length of it depends on how reliant you are of glucose and how well your body accepts this new fuel source.

Ketosis is an altered, but still natural, metabolic state that occurs either over a prolonged period of fasting or by restricting carbohydrate intake significantly, usually up to less than 50 grams per day [i].

After an overnight fast already, our liver glycogen stores will be depleted and *Captain Liver* starts to produce more ketone bodies. This, in return, will increase the availability of fatty acids in the blood stream which the body then begins to utilize for the production of energy. It can be derived from both food and the adipose tissue.

This process is called beta-oxidation. When fat is broken down by the liver, glycerol and fatty acid molecules are released. The fatty acid gets broken down even more through ketogenesis that produces a ketone body called acetoacetate. This is then converted further into two other type of ketone bodies. (1) Beta-hydroxybutyrate (BHB), which is the preferred fuel source for the brain and (2) acetone, that can be metabolized into glucose, but is mainly excreted as waste.

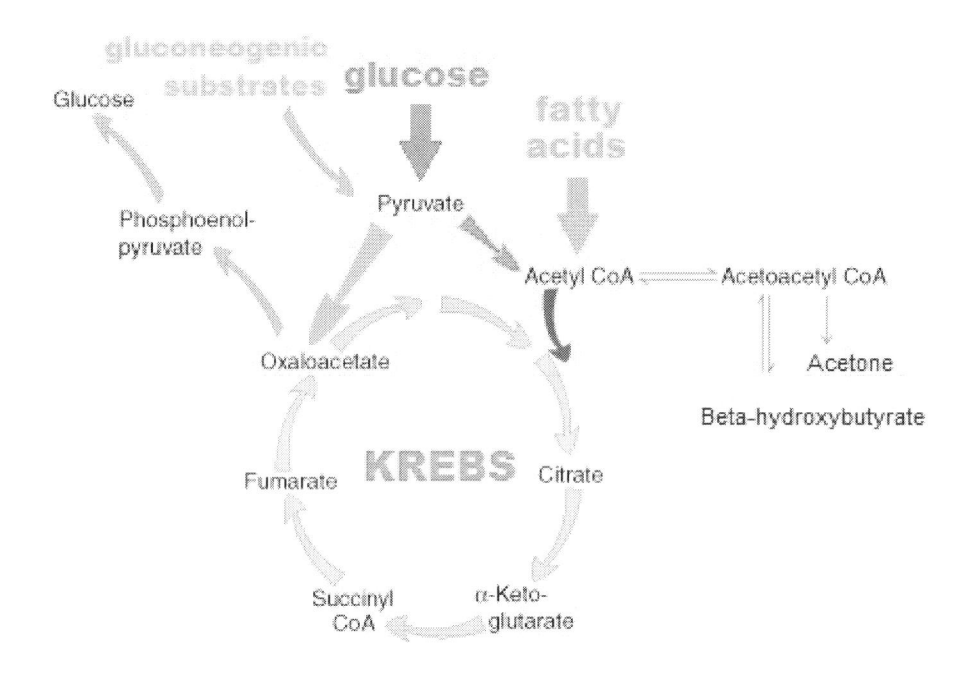

When you're running on glucose you go down the pathway of glycolysis and create pyruvate. All of these actions get burned inside the mitochondria and you can get 25% more energy from using beta-hydroxybutyrate as fuel. In this scenario of fat utilization, we're taking the more efficient route that increases the density of our cellular power plants.

Achieving the Optimal Fat Burning State

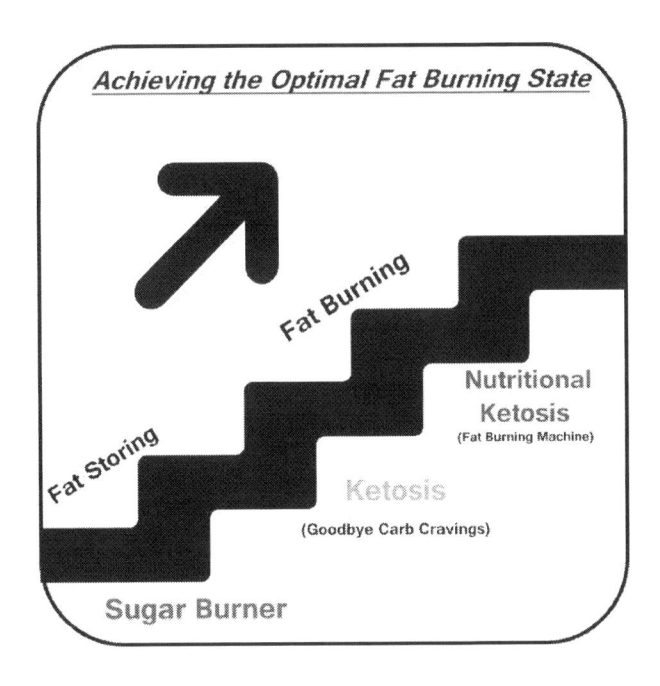

- Sugar Burner
- Fat Storing
- Ketosis (Goodbye Carb Cravings)
- Fat Burning
- Nutritional Ketosis (Fat Burning Machine)

Nutritional ketosis is not the same as ketoacidosis, which causes the pH levels in the blood to drop and become acidic. This can result with a coma and eventually death. Usually, the body manages to maintain the acidity of the blood within a normal range despite the presence of ketones. Ketoacidosis occurs mostly with type-1 diabetes and excessive alcohol consumption.

The shift from burning sugar and becoming fat adapted causes a lot of changes in your physiology. After the initial period of adaptation, the body's biochemistry will be completely altered. Approximately 75% of the energy used by the brain will be provided by ketones and the liver will change its enzymes from dominantly digesting carbohydrates to actually preferring fat [ii]. Protein catabolism decreases significantly, as fat stores are mobilized and the use of ketones increases. Muscle glycogen gets used even less and the majority of our caloric demands will be derived from the adipose tissue.

Nutritional ketosis is perfectly safe and a great metabolic state to be in.This process is an adaptive response and completely normal. During periods of famine it will enable us to survive and maintain our vitality. If we the body doesn't know how to use its stored fat for fuel, it would perish, once it runs out of sugar.

Indigenous Ketogenic Societies

Over the course of history, most aboriginal tribes have subsisted solely on high fat diets. In environments where there aren't many plants to be found, people rely primarily on meat.

The Innuit and Eskimos have lived off whale blubber, seal meat, salmon, cheese and caribou meat for centuries. Fat is their most precious commodity, as it gives them the extra calories they need to survive in such harsh climate. In fact, rent on land in some places is paid with butter. Despite that high amount of saturated fat and cholesterol in their diet, heart disease, diabetes and cancer were largely unknown. Only after they came in contact with white man's white refined carbohydrates did other diseases of the civilization catch up with them and they got obese.

The Masai tribe in Africa also follows a ketogenic diet. They're pastoralists and subsist mainly on their cattle, by eating their meat, drinking their unpasteurized milk and raw milk. Masai warriors are definitely a lot healthier and fitter than the majority of the people in our society.

Even in the Western world there are nations who eat a ton of fat. The Mediterranean Diet is thought to be the healthiest of them all. It consists of mainly fish, olive oil, cheese and vegetables. People from this region have less heart disease and better blood markers. Researchers from the States figured that it had to do with the low amount of saturated fat and cholesterol in their food. However, the Greek Orthodox Church also preaches a lot of fasting, which has even more profound health benefits. In fact, the more religious folk fast more than 200 days a year. This is the real cause for their vitality. As this ancient healing practice gets less popular amongst young people, disease begins to rise again because there are still a lot of refined grains and carbohydrates in the diet.

Is Ketosis Safe

One fear that ordinary physicians have about the ketogenic diet is that it can't sustain healthy functioning of an organism. Apart from developing ketoacidosis you'll also starve to death, which is false. How will your body and brain survive if there are no carbohydrates?

An essential nutrient is something that's required for normal physiological functioning and the survival of the organism[iii]. It cannot be synthesized by the body and thus has to be obtained from a dietary source. Carbohydrates are non-essential, unlike amino acids and fatty acids, which we don't actually need to live and can function very well without.

Amino acids and fat are essential building blocks of all the cells in our body. Protein is used to create new muscle tissue, whereas the lipids balance our hormones that instigate these processes in the first place and protect cell membrane.

The biggest reason why we have to consume so many calories every single day is to feed our hungry brain. It comprises less than 5% of our body weight but demands about 20% of our total energy expenditure. To maintain stable blood sugar levels and a caloric balance, it needs to have access to fuel all of the time.

The brain can use only about 120 grams of glucose a day [iv], which means you still need at least 30 grams of glucose while running on max ketones. That doesn't mean it ought to come from dietary carbohydrates.

During a process called *gluconeogenesis* (creation of new sugar), the liver converts amino acids found in food and glycerol, which is the backbone of triglycerides, into glucose. While in a deep fasted state, glycerol can contribute up to 21.6% of glucose production [v]. It's estimated that about 200 grams of glucose can be manufactured daily by the liver and kidneys from dietary protein and fat intake [vi].

Once you keto-adapt, your body and brain won't even need that much glucose, as they will happily use ketones instead. Carbohydrates are the default fuel source but not because they're better than fatty acids by any means. The body simply prefers it because it's easy to store and quick to absorb.

However, the brain is made up of 60% fat and runs a lot better on ketones. In fact, the high amounts of fat found in animal products and meat were probably one of the driving forces of our increased brain size. According to the Expansive Tissue Hypothesis posed by the anthropologists Leslie Aiello and Peter Wheeler suggests that the metabolic requirements of large brains were offset by a corresponding reduction of the gut[vii]. As our stomachs got smaller, our neocortices got larger. By eating solely plant foods, we wouldn't have managed to get enough excess energy for our neural network to improve itself.

In ketosis, the brain begins to use less glucose and the small amount it needs can be derived from ketogenic foods. Muscles begin to release less glycogen as well and the entire body starts using ketones for fuel. It makes the entire organism more efficient and powerful.

The Most Relevant Hormones

In the context of the cyclical ketogenic diet there are also some relevant hormones that we need to know about. What makes our plan work is the correct manipulation and expression of our biology.

- **Insulin** is the key hormone when it comes to the storage and distribution of nutrients within the body. If it is elevated, then we are more prone to store the food we eat whether into fat or muscle cells. When it is low we start to rely more on our own adipose tissue for fuel. Insulin gets released by the pancreas in response to the rise of blood sugar and tries to bring it back to normal to prevent hyperglycemia (too high blood sugar levels) or hypoglycemia (too low). It is most significantly caused by the consumption of high-glycemic carbohydrates, very little by protein or fibrous vegetables and not at all by fat. In the case of insulin sensitivity, we're quite efficient with regulating this hormone and don't need a lot to shuttle nutrients into our cells. If we're resistant, however, we can't bring it back down and will have constantly elevated levels of it, which can lead to obesity, diabetes and cardiovascular disease.

IMPORTANCE OF INSULIN

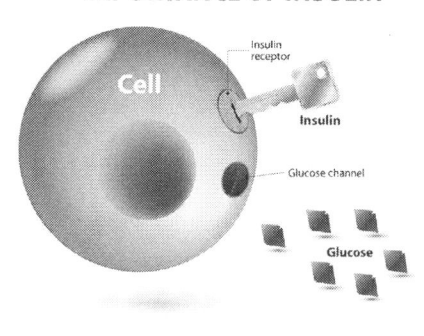

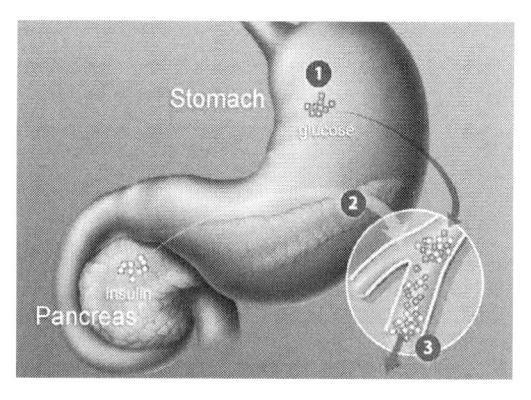

- **Leptin** regulates the feeling of satiety and hunger. Its role is to signal our brain to eat to prevent starvation. However, if we're resistant to it then the lines of communication will be cut short and our mind will never get the information that the body has received enough calories. In that case, your body is satisfied but your brain is still starving and keeps on craving for more food. It usually goes hand in hand with insulin resistance, as it is caused by the consumption of simple carbohydrates and sugar with a lot of fat at the same time.

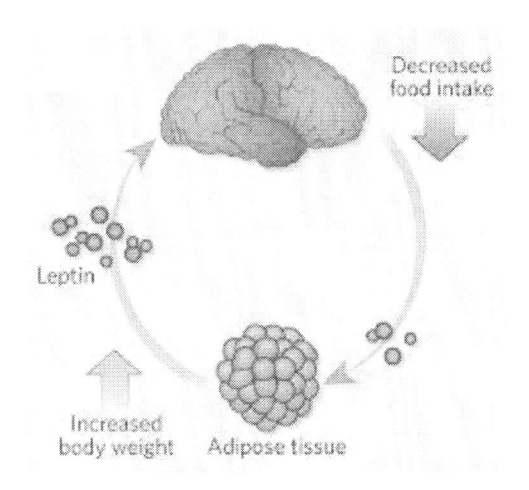

- **Ghrelin** is the hormone that creates hunger in the first place. It gets released when our stomach is empty indicating that it wants to eat something.

- **Glucagon** is the counterpart of insulin and also gets produced by the pancreas. It gets released when the concentration of glucose in the blood stream gets too low. The liver then starts to convert stored glycogen into glucose.

- **Serotonin** is a neurotransmitter primarily found in the gastrointestinal tract and the central nervous system of animals. It's also considered to be the relaxation hormone which contributes to the feeling of well-being and happiness. Proteins contain an amino acid called tryptophan that gets converted into serotonin in the brain. Carbohydrates can also release serotonin.

- **Human growth hormone (HGH)** stimulates growth and cell development within the body. Its role is to produce and regenerate the organism's tissue and has anabolic effects because it raises the concentration of glucose and free fatty acids in the blood stream. Children have a lot of it because they're constantly growing. For adults this hormone increases muscle building and fat burning. It's the Holy Grail for longevity, high end performance and excellent body composition.

- **Insulin-like growth factor (IGF-1)** is a hormone that plays a crucial part in childhood growth and also has anabolic effects in adults as well. It is one of the most effective natural activators of pathways responsible for cellular growth and inhibitor of cellular death. IGF-1 is closely connected with HGH. The release of HGH into the blood stream by the anterior pituitary gland also stimulates the liver to produce IGF-1 which causes systemic growth in almost every cell in the body, especially muscle, cartilage, bone, liver, kidney, nerves, skin and lungs. It can also nerve cell growth and development. Currently research is not clear about whether or not IGF-1 signaling is positively or negatively associated with aging and cancer. Over-expression may lead to cancer but on the other hand natural enhanced actions of HGH and IGF-1 are effective ways of establishing an anabolic state, supporting the immune system.

- **Testosterone** is associated with masculine behavior but it's also found in women as well. This is yet another anabolic hormone that enhances muscle building and strength but also has some cognitive benefits. Too low levels of it will decrease reproductive functions, cause fat storage and increase risk of cardiovascular disease. The best T-boosters are heavy resistance training, high intensity interval training (HIIT), dietary fat intake and proper sleep. Maintaining a straight posture and not slumping over will also release testosterone because of the powerful feeling and confidence we get.

- **Cortisol,** also known as the main stress and "fight or flight" hormone, controls our energy in strenuous circumstances. Evolutionarily, its role is to enable us to survive in situations of life and death. It gets elevated when we would have to run away from a lion, fight off a pack of wolves, while drowning or chasing after dinner. As a result, glucose gets released into the blood stream to provide more energy so that we could escape danger. The body perceives every type of stress response as the same and sitting in traffic, being nervous about public speaking, exercising hard or arguing with someone release as much cortisol as fighting a tiger would. Occasional short spikes of stress are necessary and can be beneficial as it conditions us to handle difficult situations. If it's elevated for too long, then anabolism and catabolism get out of balance leading to decreased levels of testosterone and excessive breakdown of tissue.

These hormones get released within us in response to the food we eat, what we do, our current condition, degree of sensitivity to them and also the time of the day. This means that we're totally in control of our own biology and can influence how they affect us and when.

The most important one is insulin, as it directs the distribution of nutrients throughout the body. It's responsible for both fat loss and muscle gain – everything concerning our body composition. That's why our main focus on the Keto cycle is to be mindful of how and when we would want to release it.

How to Get into Ketosis

To induce ketosis insulin needs to be suppressed for an extended period of time. As a result, glucagon goes up and starts to empty the liver's glycogen stores.

This is achieved by using our current storage and not eating high glycemic carbohydrates that raise our blood sugar even before we can put them into our mouth. Protein does so as well but to a much lesser degree and more steadily. Add fat into the mix and it will happen even more slowly. Leafy green vegetables are also safe as the actual amount of sugar in them is small in comparison to their fiber content, which decreases the rate of absorption.

The macronutrient ratios of the standard ketogenic diet (SKD) are 70-80% fat, 15-25% protein and <5% NET carbs.

CALORIE BREAKDOWN

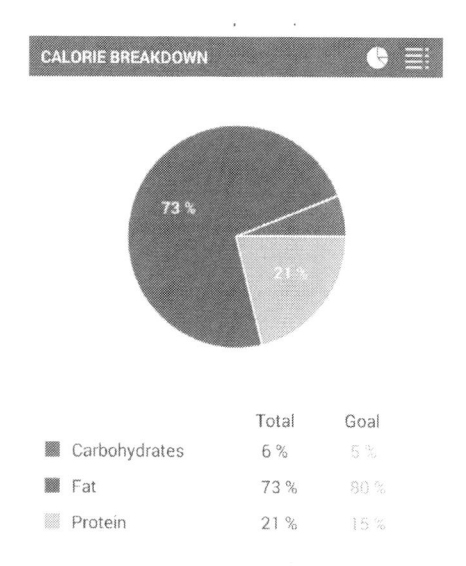

	Total	Goal
Carbohydrates	6 %	5 %
Fat	73 %	80 %
Protein	21 %	15 %

Nutritional ketosis alters our metabolism completely and makes us use various fuel sources completely differently. **Keto adaptation increases the rate at which the body burns saturated fat for fuel and maintains better overall glucose levels.**

The list of foods eaten on a ketogenic diet.

Carbohydrates.

Total caloric proportion is less than 5 %. In total, the carbohydrate intake would be around 30 grams, fiber not included. The less of them, the faster will ketosis be induced.

Safe sources are fibrous leafy green and cruciferous vegetables, including mushrooms and some nightshade.

Food	Amount	Fat	NET Carbs (g)	Protein (g)
Lettuce, Butterhead	2oz/56 grams	0	0.5	1
Beet Greens	2oz/56 grams	0	0.5	1
Bok Choy	2oz/56 grams	0	0.5	1
Spinach	2oz/56 grams	0	1	1.5
Alfalfa Sprouts	2oz/56 grams	0	1	2
Swiss Chard	2oz/56 grams	0	1	1

Arugula	2oz/56 grams	0	1	1.5
Celery	2oz/56 grams	0	1	0.5
Lettuce	2oz/56 grams	0	1	0.5
Asparagus	2oz/56 grams	0	1	1
Eggplant	2oz/56 grams	0	1	0.5
Mushrooms, White	2oz/56 grams	0	1.5	2
Tomatoes	2oz/56 grams	0	1	0.5
Cauliflower	2oz/56 grams	0	1.5	1

Green Bell Pepper	2oz/56 grams	0	1.5	0.5
Cabbage	2oz/56 grams	0	2	1
Broccoli	2oz/56 grams	0	2	1.5
Green Beans	2oz/56 grams	0	2	1
Brussels Sprouts	2oz/56 grams	0	2.5	1.5
Kale	2oz/56 grams	0	2	2
Artichoke	2oz/56 grams	0	2.5	2
Kelp	2oz/56 grams	0	3	1

Zucchini	2oz/56 grams	0	2	1

There are also a small variety of fruits and berries you can consume.

Food	Amount	Fat (g)	NET Carbs (g)	Protein (g)
Rhubarb	100 grams	0	2	1
Raspberries	100 grams	0	5	1.5
Blueberries	100 grams	0	10	2
Strawberries	100 grams	0	5	1
Blackberries	100 grams	0	5	1.5

Top 5 recommendations are:

- Spinach
- Kelp
- Broccoli
- Cauliflower
- Cabbage

Protein

Total caloric proportion at about 15 %. Careful not to consume lean bits without any fat to slow down the absorption as it might get converted into sugar. The body will always try to find glucose. During the adaptation phase it will happen more easily than later. Pure protein with nothing else will go through glyconeogenesis (creation of new sugar). Best stick to fatty chunks.

Meat is obviously one of the best source.

Food	Amount	Fat (g)	NET Carbs (g)	Protein
Pork Chops	100 grams	14	0	24
Chicken Drumstick	1 medium drumstick	8	0	9
Chicken Wing	1 medium drumstick	7	0	8

Food	Amount	Fat (g)	NET Carbs (g)	Protein
Bacon	100 grams	42	0	37
Beef, Ground	100 grams	15	0	26
Lamb and Mutton	100 grams	21	0	25
Venison	100 grams	5	0	31
Liver, mammalian, fowl	100 grams	5	4	26
Duck	100 grams	28	0	19
Wild Boar	100 grams	4	0	28

Additionally, fatty fish, such as

Food	Amount	Fat (g)	NET Carbs (g)	Protein
Salmon	100 grams	13	0	20

Sardines	100 grams	13	0	25
Herring	100 grams	9	0	18
Mackerel	100 grams	25	0	19
Anchovies	100 grams	10	0	29
Sprats	100 grams	15	0	20

The best source of protein are probably eggs. They have the entire amino acid profile and are full of omega-3s, DHA, EPA and cholesterol, which is great for the cells and brain. Nutrition of 1 large egg: 5 grams of fat, 1 gram of carbs, 6 grams of protein.

However, some caution needs to be taken. All of those things can't be taken equally. Some pre-packaged products have added sugar in them and under many names (dextrose, glucose, fructose, maltodextrin, xylitol etc.) all of which ought to be avoided for best results.

Top 5 recommendations are:

- Eggs

- Salmon
- Beef
- Pork
- Chicken

Fats

To be honest, there isn't actually a limit to how much fat we should be consuming. The more of it, the more ketones will be produced. With no carbohydrates in the menu we need to have another fuel source for the body.

In order to get into ketosis, we need to eat fat and a lot of it. What I'm talking about is adding it on our vegetables, protein, coffee - everywhere.

Food	Amount	Fat (g)	NET Carbs (g)	Protein
Butter	28 grams/1oz	28	0	0
Ghee	28 grams/1oz	28	0	0

Lard	28 grams/1oz	28	0	0
Tallow	28 grams/1oz	28	0	0
Avocado Oil	28 grams/1oz	28	0	0
Cocoa Butter	28 grams/1oz	28	0	0
Coconut Oil	28 grams/1oz	28	0	0
Flaxseed Oil	28 grams/1oz	28	0	0
Macadamia Oil	28 grams/1oz	28	0	0
MCT Oil	28 grams/1oz	28	0	0
Olive Oil	28 grams/1oz	28	0	0
Red Palm	28	28	0	0

Oil	grams/1oz			
Coconut Cream	28 grams/1oz	10	1	1
Olives	28 grams/1oz	4	0.5	1
Avocados	28 grams/1oz	4	2	1
Coconut Milk	28 grams/1oz	7	1	1
Almond Butter	28 grams/1oz	18	2	7
Brazil Nuts	28 grams/1oz	19	1	4
Heavy Cream, Full Fat	28 grams/1oz	10	1	1
Cheese, Cheddar	28 grams/1oz	9	1	7
Cheese,	28	8	1	6

| Blue | grams/1oz | | | |

What ought to be avoided are refined vegetable oils and trans fats, such as rapeseed oil, canola oil, margarine etc. They are more inflammatory and actually dangerous for our health. Also, the biggest reason why saturated fat is considered bad in the first place.

Top 5 recommendations are:

- MCT Oil

- Organic Extra Virgin Coconut Oil

- Extra Virgin Olive Oil

- Premium Avocado Oil

- Grass-Fed Butter

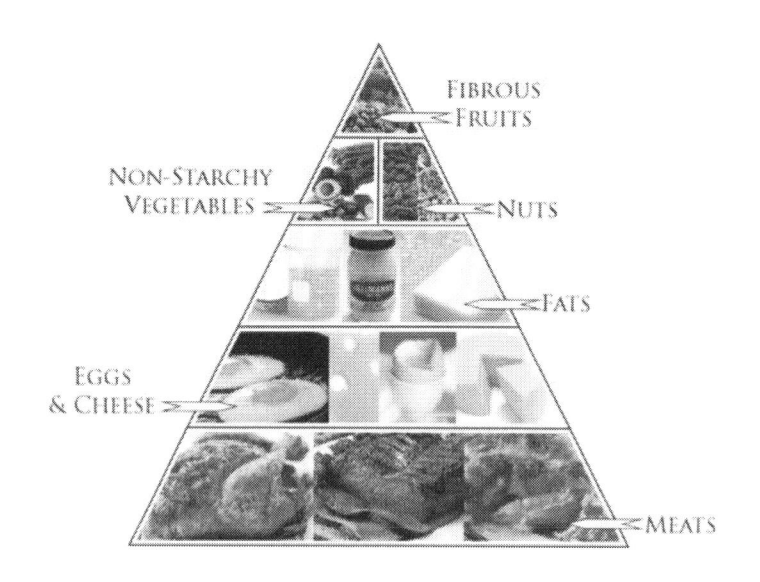

How to Know You Are in Ketosis

The process of adaptation takes at least 2-3 weeks. At first, you won't be able to experience almost any of the benefits, but will suffer from withdrawal symptoms.

This "keto flu" happens because the body doesn't know how to use fat for fuel. The brain will be screaming for energy and demands glucose. Eating carbs will put a cold halt to inducing ketosis and prevents any metabolic change.

This is where patience and perseverance come into play. The severity of it will depend on how addicted to sugar your body has been before. If you come from the background of the standard American diet (SAD), then it will take you longer than someone who is used to eating Paleo and already used to less sugar.

During that period there will be some uncomfortable signs of withdrawal, such as dizziness, fatigue, slight headaches and the feeling of being hit with a club, which all pass away after a while.

To know whether or not you're in ketosis you can measure your blood ketones using Ketostix. Optimal measurements are between 0,5 and 3,0 mMol-s. The same can be done with a glucometer. If you're fasting blood glucose is under 80 mg/dl and you're not feeling hypoglycemic then you're probably in ketosis. Ketoacidocis occurs over 10mMol-s, which is quite hard to reach.

What level of Ketosis is optimal?

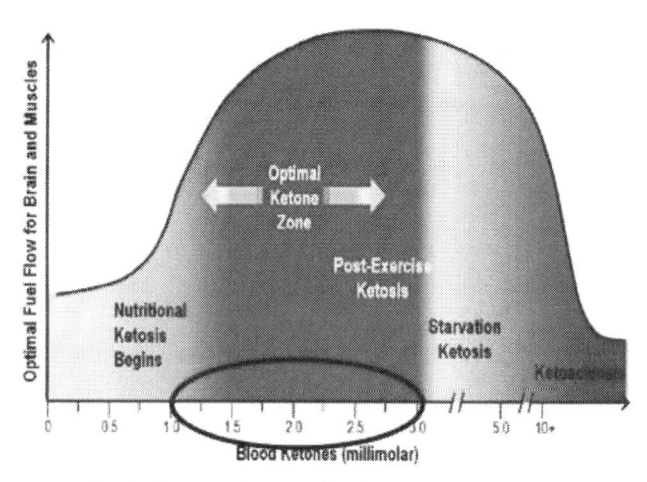

Page 91: The Art and Science of Low Carbohydrate Performance
Jeff S. Volek and Stephen D. Phinney

BLOOD GLUCOSE CHART

Mg/DL	Fasting	After Eating	2-3 hours After Eating
Normal	80-100	170-200	120-140
Impaired Glucose	101-125	190-230	140-160
Diabetic	126+	220-300	200 plus

Additional symptoms during adaptation include:

- Water weight loss. Your body will be completely flushed from carbs.
- Increased thirst. Because of the same reason. Drink more water than normally.

- The Keto breath. Acetone, the ketone body leaves a metallic taste in your mouth and an acidic or "fruity" smell.
- Stinky urine. You're excreting acetone again. Your sweat may also smell.
- Slight headaches and fatigue. The brain is in an energy crisis that will be shortly overcome.
- Lack of appetite. No hunger because of using fat for fuel.

After adaptation you'll experience:

- No hunger whatsoever.
- Mental clarity.
- High levels of energy at all times.
- Increased endurance.
- Reduced inflammation
- Reduced bloating.
- No sugar cravings.
- Improved sleep.
- Stable blood sugar levels.
- No muscle catabolism.

- Less fatigue during exercise, any other time as well, really.

This is what to expect once you've become fat adapted. You can use Ketostix to measure your progress. But it doesn't necessarily mean you're in ketosis *per se*. Follow your intuition first and foremost.

On the Keto Cycle it doesn't matter whether or not you're in ketosis. It's not a magic pill that immediately turns you into a superhuman. Nor is it a badge of honor that you could wear. *"Oh, look at me, I'm precisely in the optimal zone of ketone bodies. Therefore, I'm better than you!"*

Unless you're diabetic or have any other medical condition, then you shouldn't worry about getting kicked out of ketosis.

Being fat adapted and burning fat for fuel is a lot more important. This can be achieved by eating low carb as well. However, the initial period of keto adaptation is necessary for these pathways to be created.

Chapter II
Why Do the Ketogenic Diet

But why should we want to enter ketosis in the first place. There are numerous benefits to this state, some of which are extremely advantageous. Most important ones are concerned with our overall health but there are also some performance enhancing ones.

The most obvious advantage is increased fat oxidation[viii]. Consuming carbohydrates will make our body secrete more insulin. When this hormone is elevated we're more prone to storing rather than burning. If it's constantly high, we'll never be able to actually tap into using our own resources. In the case of body composition, it's the most important hormone there is, as it directly controls how we're using our food. High carb diets make lipase, the enzyme involved in breaking down body fat, almost completely inactive.

By aiming for ketosis and continuing to train in it, we're conditioning ourselves to become more efficient with our inner fuel supplies. It's the greatest strategy of self-resourcefulness there is, as we'll be independent of food and will be able to perform in any situation under any circumstances. Imagine yourself being like an aboriginal hunter-gatherer or an ancient warrior who's able to spearhead mammoths, kill sabertooth tigers, wrestle bears and fight battles for hours upon end.

When you're running on glucose you go down the pathway of glycolysis and create pyruvate. All of these actions get burned inside the mitochondria and you can get 25% more energy from using beta-hydroxybutyrate as fuel.

The by-products of glucose metabolism are advanced glycation end-products (AGEs), which promote inflammation and oxidative stress[ixx], by binding a protein or lipid molecule with sugar. They speed up aging[xi], and can cause diabetes. This doesn't happen when burning clean fuel - quality fat. Also, the constantly elevated levels of circulating blood sugar are associated with nerve malfunctioning, high morbidity, bacterial infection, cancer progression and Alzheimer's.

The #1 food for tumors is sugar. Eating keto foods, prevents the accumulation of excess glucose in the blood, which leads to the cellular suicide of cancer. With no carbohydrates for it to feed upon, it will potentially disappear completely, at least it will diminish in size. At the same time, your healthy cells will still be nourished because they'll be using fat.

Ketosis reduces natural hunger to a bare minimum and regulates appetite[xii]. This is the result of the body being able to generate energy from both the adipose tissue and dietary fat intake. The ability to go without meals for 24 hours while not suffering any stomach pains or carb driven cravings of insanity is incredibly empowering, not to mention useful for both fitness and reducing fat composition.

Our body is made to burn fat. The adipose tissue is like a black hole with infinite storage capacity. Any surplus calorie we don't need right away gets deposited for future use. When in ketosis, we'll be withdrawing energy from our own body fat to maintain a caloric balance.

Ketones are the "superfuel" above both glucose and free fatty acids. As you can remember, they can produce 25% more energy and will cover 75% of the brains energy demands. When in ketosis you begin to need less and less glucose, which makes you more and more self-reliant.

Ketosis for Health

Because of the fact that a fat molecule has twice the amount of calories than a carbohydrate it gets digested a lot slower. **Unlike sugar, that gets burned up easily, ketones move steadily and provide long lasting energy.**

This also prevents any rise in blood sugar from taking place, which happens after consuming something with a high glycemic index. Instant bursts of energy will inevitably fall as quickly. What goes up must come down. This results in hypoglycemia (a crash of blood sugar) and sleepiness. With fat that doesn't happen as we will have an abundant fuel source thus always feeling great. Instead of secreting insulin and taking our bodies for a rollercoaster ride we maintain a steady stream.

Following a low carbohydrate high fat diet has been proven very effective against a lot of the chronic illnesses people struggle with.

- Reduction in triglycerides[xiii]
- Increase in HDL cholesterol (the good one)[xiv]

- Drop in blood pressure[xv] and insulin levels[xvi]

All of which prevent heart disease, diabetes and metabolic syndrome[xvii]. For optimal health it looks very appealing.

Mark my words when I say that ketosis will help to cure cancer in the near future, as it's already being used as effective treatment. At the moment science is just beginning to fully understand and utilize this metabolic state.

Athletes Going Against the Grain (Pun Intended)

If you're physically active and fit, then you probably don't have to worry about obesity and other ailments. However, this doesn't mean that you can't pick up any disease or develop a severe medical condition.

Insulin resistance happens in the case of consuming too many simple carbohydrates and being constantly on a blood sugar rollercoaster ride. Even the most athletic of individuals can become diabetic and a lot of professional athletes already have.

Following a low carb diet while still training ought to optimize our health first and foremost. However, there are also a lot of performance enhancing benefits to using fat for fuel.

The maximum amount of glucose our bodies can store is about 2000 calories (approximately 400-500 grams of carbohydrates in the muscles, 100-150 grams in the liver and about 15 grams in the blood). Once this runs out, more fatty acids are produced to supply the demand. Although this is the point in which adipose tissue is being used it only happens to a certain degree. To still get some form of glucose, the body will also begin to break down a bit of the protein in muscles and organs to create sugar. The reason is that it's not that adapted to primarily using ketones. To prevent that from happening, a person would need to be constantly adding in more carbohydrates to fuel their activities.

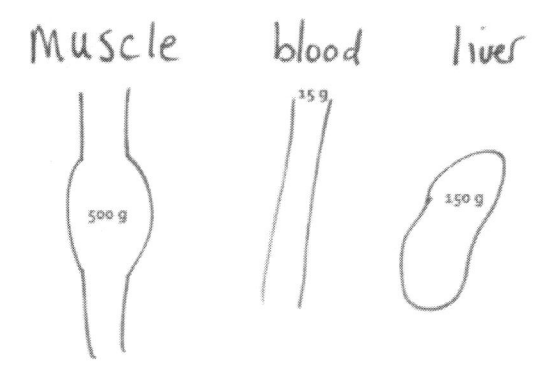

In ketosis, however, the main source of energy is significantly bigger. **Even the leanest of people with 7 % body fat carry around more than 20 000 worth of calories with them at all times.** Refeeding isn't necessary as there is always some fuel available. This also preserves muscles and other vital organs from being catabolized. Instead of being a quick sugar burner we can become efficient fat burners instead.

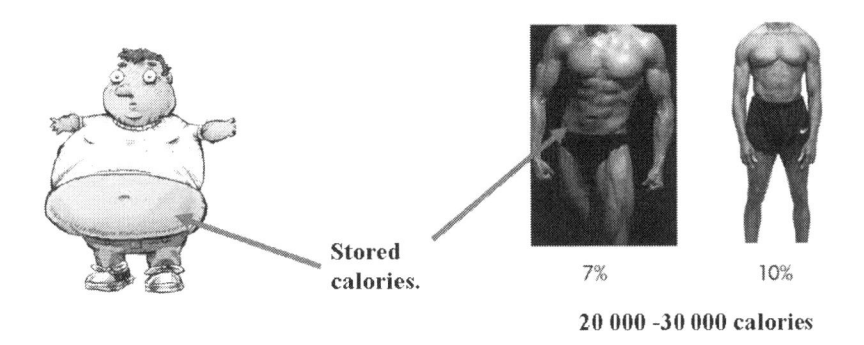

Stored calories.

7%   10%

20 000 -30 000 calories

Ketogenic dieting is becoming very popular amongst endurance athletes, especially ultra-runners and ironman triathletes who have to perform at a high level for extreme durations. By carrying around their own fuel on their bodies they can tap into an abundance of energy. They literally go against the grain of everything in optimal sport's nutrition.

For instance, Sami Inkinen and his wife Meredith Loring rowed across the Pacific Ocean from California to Hawaii in

45 days, while following a low-carb, sugar-free, high-fat ketogenic diet. Despite being physically active for 21 hours a day, they did not suffer any decrease in performance, health or cravings for carbs. Such adaptation shows that we are capable of a lot more than we actually think. How else did our ancestors complete their epic journeys of exploration and migration across the globe?

In a study on advanced triathletes the group who followed a ketogenic approach instead of the traditional high-carb diet showed 2-3 times higher peak fat oxidation during submaximal exercise[xviii].

Contrary to popular belief physical performance does not suffer by ditching the carbs. It is also used in strength sports such as powerlifting and gymnastics[xix] where the intensities are lot higher. Bodybuilders use periods of low-carb eating to prepare for shows and improve body composition.

There are very few people who have stayed and trained in ketosis for several years. The most well-known ketogenic bodybuilder is Luis Villasenor, aka *Darthluiggi,* who has been on keto since 2001 and has made some impressive natural gains over the course of more than 15 years. He's also the leading figure of reddit.com's Ketogains community.

In my own experience, I haven't noticed any negative side-effects of ketosis after proper adaptation. I have managed to improve every aspect of my training and health. It definitely feels great and is well worth the effort.

When you're trying to achieve peak physical performance and pushing your body to the extreme, what do you think is holding you back the most? Your muscles? Heart? Blood vessels? Lungs? Joints? Well, to a certain extent all of them, as you need to have a well-functioning physiology across all domains. But the biggest influence lies between your ears.

One of the reason for *"bonking"* and *hitting the wall* during exercise is that your brain gets fatigued, not your muscles. Ever heard the saying that *once you feel like quitting, you've only reached 40% of your potential*? That's what Navy SEALs are saying. This is the truth, because our mind will always try to prevent us from exerting ourselves too much.

From the perspective of evolutionary psychology, we're predisposed to preserve and store energy – to move very little and accumulate as much fat as possible. Our body isn't very interested in building muscle. Strength and endurance might come in handy, but we're not meant to be exerting ourselves in any shape or from.

Reaching exhaustion and building up too much lactic acid in the muscles (the burn effect) is caused by limited blood circulation. In the mitochondria this process is called *anaerobiosis*, which prevents the oxidative removal of lactic acid. This is influenced by the size of your blood vessels and heart, but the initial command to trigger <u>this mechanism originates from the central governor inside our head.</u>

This issue can be overcome by tricking or distracting your mind so that you can lift heavier, run faster, go harder and longer. Simple techniques include counting numbers to 20 or 50 over and over again or concentrating on an intermediate goal just ahead, like the next sign post or chunking down long periods (like 30 minutes) into smaller 5-minute bouts. Listening to driving music that pumps you up will also put you into beast mode. Positive affirmations, self-talk and even mental visualization will narrow down your focus on the task at hand and unleashes your inner predator as well.

The reason why our brain starts to fight back at us is that it runs out of oxygen and experiences sustained periods of hypoxia (low levels of oxygen), which can cause death or permanently damage your organs. Our *"Central Governor"* thus limits how hard we can go by reducing the nervous system's recruitment of muscle fibers, which causes the perceived sensation of fatigue. Suddenly, it simply says *STOP!* and your body listens to it.

If you're attempting to overcome this exhaustion by continuing to push yourself, then the mind will also eventually reach decision fatigue. Our first priority in any situation is to maintain homeostasis and inner equilibrium. This energy crisis happens because the body has run out of its endogenous fuel, *i.e. glycogen.* Once you become fat adapted you won't hit the wall because there is none to be found. Your body will use less glycogen and the mind has a steady stream to calories, thus maintaining its functioning.

Some marathon runners literally cross the finish line in tears, because they simply have so much willpower which enables them to push past any feeling of exhaustion and even physical pain. They literally wreck their bodies into ruins. It's admirable, but foolish. When using a ketogenic fuel tank, this perceived fatigue rarely happens thanks to solving the energy crisis.

Keto Smart

In addition to performance oriented benefits ketosis also has cognitive and mental ones. There's a big difference between being high on keto versus sugar.

Because of how evolutionarily valuable glucose is, the brain's reward endorphin system lights up every time we consume it, making us want more. We release a lot of the "feel-good" chemicals, such as dopamine and serotonin. Cravings and hunger pains come from some people's mind kicking into overdrive and losing their reason over something sweet.

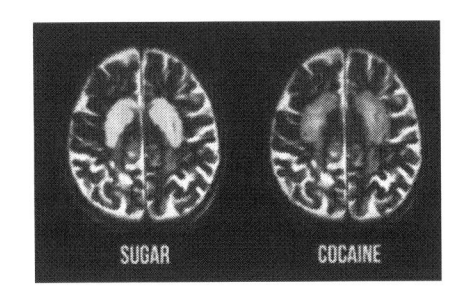

As you can see, the brain's reward system lights up the same way on sugar as it does on hard drugs. In neurological terms, binge eating and drug addiction are the same thing[xx].

This happens so that we would be motivated to repeat our actions in the future. Our taste buds are designed to recognize sweetness and fire up every single time. Feeling good after eating something sugary puts us on a short high and makes us want more.

Sugar cravings are caused by an energy crisis in the body. If the brain doesn't get access to fuel, it will try to motivate you to find something to eat. Because by default it only knows how to use glucose, it will also expect to have it.

However, if you've plugged into your largest fuel tank, your own body fat, then you won't experience these cravings. That's why people lose their sweet tooth completely when on a low carb diet. Their body detoxifies itself from sugar and the mind will get clearer.

Sugar doesn't actually provide us with that much energy and is mainly an illusion. It's a way of trapping our own ATP production. We might have a lot of stored calories but we won't be able to access them. This leads to *mental bonking* and *physical exhaustion* in everything you do, whether that be training, reading or anything else. That's why it's important to go through keto adaptation to teach the body how to use fat for fuel.

By avoiding carbohydrates, we also avoid the ups and downs of blood sugar, thus allowing our brain to function properly. By having a steady stream of energy it doesn't have to be on the lookout for glucose. Some is indeed needed, which gets created by the liver, but the majority can be derived from ketones. This type of eating has been used to cure children of epilepsy and is now being studied for other disorders as well, such as Alzheimer's and Parkinson's disease.

With the brain satisfied, our cognition has the opportunity to flourish. This allows us to maintain mental clarity and avoid mind fog, which accompanies the consumption of whole grains. The majority of the brain is made up of fat (60%), and the more you eat it, the better it can function. After keto adaptation, this precious organ will derive up to 75% of its energy demands from ketones. The minute amount of glucose will be created by the liver and derived from those few carbohydrates you'll be getting from food.

On a fat burning metabolism, we can think more clearly and with less disruption. Our ability to concentrate increases and I dare say that so does our intelligence. Who knows, maybe our IQ does so as well. Not directly, but as a result of being able to allocate our psychic energy into appropriate channels and activities that make us smarter. Our focus during training will definitely be acute. Personally, I've definitely noticed a lot of improvement in this area.

Sleep Like the Sleeping Beauty

Additionally, the quality of our sleep improves because of the stability in blood sugar. If we run out of glucose in the middle of the night, then we will become hypoglycemic. Our starving brain will wake us up to get some fuel for survival. Midnight snacking is another example of people feeding all of the time and a bad habit to have.

Constant stream of energy means that there's no need to recharge as much, resulting in quality slumber. This way we can go through full sleep cycles and actually enter the deepest stages of recovery where all dreaming occurs and the magic happens. During my own periods of ketosis, I've gone through the entire night like a log without waking up.

Sleep is one of the most important things for building muscle, getting stronger and burning fat. During the day we're exposing our body to all types of exhausting activities that push our limits to the extreme. Weightlifting, intense intervals, deadlifts, mental algorithms, situational awareness, cognitive sharpness etc. are all draining us and not something we're supposed to be facing with on a daily basis. To actually cause enhanced physiological adaptations we have to allow the recovery processes to happen.

What you will also see is that you get less tired overall when on keto. Physical activities become less demanding and your endurance will increase by default. If you're obese, then you'll reclaim your enthusiasm and vitality for life.

Once you go through the shift and eat appropriately, your body will heal itself. Inflammation disappears and you'll have less aches and pains. You may think that it's normal to be feeling the way you do now, but that's because you don't know that there's another way.

All of these benefits are the reason why you should try a ketogenic diet... at least once. It will give you high end physical as well as cognitive performance and is incredibly healthy.

Being in this metabolic state is very advantageous, as we become more resourceful with our own supplies and can thus always be excelling at whatever we're doing. You're going to have to keep it a secret, but the military is also very interested of ketosis and is actively testing it on topnotch soldiers. When on keto, we literally can become Superhuman.

Chapter III
Return of the Carbohydrate Paradigm Shift

Ketosis is a powerful tool and an advantageous metabolic state to be in. For overall health and well-being, it's perfect and sustainable. In comparison to a high carbohydrate one, the standard ketogenic diet (SKD) definitely has more health benefits.

Despite that, there are still some shortcomings that might occur.

Mineral deficiencies are the cause of our food not being as nutritious as it used to be in the first place, in addition to the low amount of variety in the diet.

Thyroid functioning can also suffer on people with a predisposing medical condition or during initial adaptation. This needs to be addressed with either a lot of iodine supplementation or a small spike of insulin that actually instigates a lot of the repair and growth mechanisms in the body because of its purely anabolic effects. It does so with both the good (muscle growth, fat burning), the bad (adipose tissue accumulation) and the ugly (cancers and tumors). Therefore, a wise person would take control of it and use this tool wisely and strategically when necessary.

Additionally, glucose is the body's primary fuel source for a reason. That's why we don't always need nor want to be in ketosis. It's perfect for endurance activities but at higher intensities isn't ideal. Muscle contractions for absolute power require some glycogen but that happens only very rarely. If you think that simple aerobics will cause that to happen then you're wrong. What I'm talking about is 110% of our VO2 max and not for short bouts but prolonged time periods. **Very intense metabolic conditioning is glycolytic and requires glycogen to be performed.**

Think of it as a boost of nitrous oxide race cars use in certain situations. Unless you refuel appropriately your metabolism will downregulate and also lower testosterone. Therefore, if you're training extremely hard then you would be better off with occasionally consuming some carbohydrates.

Moreover, glucose promotes muscle growth and other forms of hormone production. Because of low levels of insulin ketones aren't as great for building new tissue, although it's possible.

For muscle growth we need 4 things:

- An adequate training stimulus (train hard and heavy)
- Protein synthesis (eat enough protein to repair the damage)
- Energy (be in a caloric surplus)
- Hormonal output (mainly testosterone and HGH)

None of those variables require the consumption of carbohydrates and can be covered even on SKD. We only need ample amounts of protein and amino acids for muscle building nutrition.

In my own experience I've managed to actually increase strength and build muscle while in ketosis, which is seemingly impossible according to widespread belief. We get bigger and stronger because of the demands we put on our body not because of what we eat *per se*.

To dispute some of the myths about training and prove to you that it's possible to build muscle and strength on keto, we have to return to the body's physiology.

By default, we're hardwired to use carbohydrates as our main fuel. This is reinforced even more by the high amounts of them in our diet. To create energy, sugar enters the Krebs cycle during the process of glycolysis. Out comes pyruvate that gets converted to ATP.

The body can store about 2000 calories of glycogen. Liver glycogen stores will be depleted already after an overnight fast. It's our first fuel tank. To release glucose from muscle cells we need a lot more. This supply is scarce and used only when there's no other way. When we would have to run from a lion or sprint after the bus.

Muscle glycogen stores get tapped into only during very intense and glycolytic activities. When in an anaerobic mode we're utilizing solely glucose for fuel to produce ATP in the presence of no oxygen.

Free fatty acids, on the other hand, are almost infinite in terms of caloric storage. We can deposit as much triglycerides in our adipose tissue as we can possibly consume.

Despite glucose being the body's primary fuel source, most of the time we're using fat for fuel. During activities with lower intensities we're being aerobic, which means that we have access to oxygen and can breathe normally. In this state we're capable of maintaining movement for longer periods of time without running into a fuel crisis.

When it comes to choosing between which energy system benefits more from ketones, then the answer is obviously the aerobic.

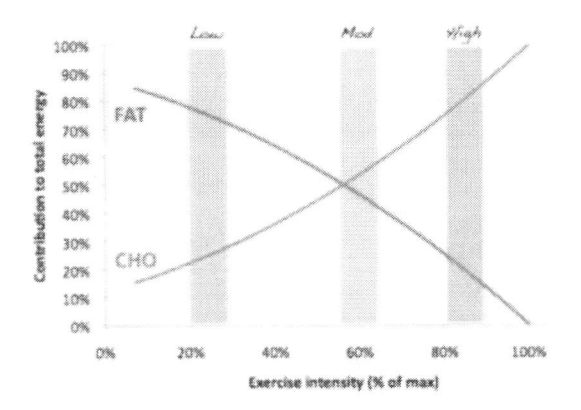

At lower intensities the body will happily use fatty acids or ketones for fuel and will spare its muscle glycogen for emergencies. That energy will be derived either from ingested dietary fat or, once we've run out of consumed calories, our own adipose tissue.

In the case of sugar burning, you'll be able to do the same, but only to a certain extent. After you've run out of immediate fuel, you're going to burn fat. But because you're mainly running on glucose, you'll also begin to break down your own tissue through gluconeogenesis. This process breaks down protein from your muscle cells and organs to convert it into sugar. It's a very inefficient way of producing energy and happens because the body doesn't know how to utilize ketones.

When in deep ketosis, you reduce muscle catabolism to a bare minimum because of being able to find an efficient solution to the energy crisis.

Unless you're fully keto adapted, your anaerobic performance will suffer slightly. If the body is still yearning for glucose, then you won't be able to use ketones at higher intensities. At least as much as your mind would like to.

However, it doesn't mean that you can't train without oxygen or sugar.

High intensity training, such as HIIT cycles, are anaerobic by nature and span the creatine-phosphate system. Past that 90% of your maximum, you're actually using glycogen quite inefficiently as well. It's just that you'll be able to produce explosive ATP faster with glucose.

After you've gone through the shift, you'll be able to spare your glycogen and can actually perform at your maximum with ketones as effectively as you would when using glucose.

Do You Need Carbs?

The popular belief is that you need carbohydrates to replenish glycogen. This seems obvious, because our muscle cells and liver can store glucose, which is sugar. If you want to restore your fuel, then eat carbs, right?

However, it's not necessary to eat carbs to refill our glycogen stores. Glycerol, which is found in triglycerides, can be turned into glycogen through the same process of gluconeogenesis. Consumption of foods with amino acids and low carb vegetables also contributes to this. It's estimated that about 200 grams of glucose can be manufactured daily by the liver and kidneys from dietary protein and fat intake [xxi]. After some time, you will be able to store glycogen even on a ketogenic diet.

However, carbs simply add the extra benefit to that and in that situation are optimal, making them more supreme for muscle growth and enhancement.

People on the SKD have reported improved strength and endurance when having some pre-workout glucose. Same reports have been found amongst people who do a lot of aerobic training on a SKD. Fatty acids and ketones are great for fuel at low intensities, but your performance is nevertheless limited by glucose and muscle glycogen. Even low carb endurance athletes can still shift into higher gear by consuming some carbohydrates around workouts.

Whatever the case might be, anyone who is following a ketogenic diet can benefit from some exogenous carbs when performing at higher intensities. If you're training hard and heavy <u>more frequently</u>, then your body won't have enough time to replenish your muscle glycogen stores solely via gluconeogenesis.

Carbohydrates and insulin are not the enemy here. The new dogma of low carb eating makes the same mistake as people did by blaming it all on fat. Of course, refined sugar and pastries are extremely bad for our health. It's just that people eat both of these macronutrients under the wrong circumstances and at random times.

Insulin is a powerful anabolic hormone that assists growth and tissue repair. It governs nutrient partitioning and influences whether or not the calories consumed go into muscle or fat cells.

The benefits to this are immense and useful, but only in a specific context – when our glycogen stores are completely empty and ready to absorb some carbohydrates. That happens after heavy resistance training, but not all of the time. The Keto Cycle takes this into account and structures our carb intake accordingly.

Even though we might be exercising it doesn't mean we're tapping into our glucose reserves. We shouldn't want to either. Because it's a vital fuel source the body will try to hold onto every gram no matter what and use it only in survival scenarios where failure is not an option – when you would have to run from a lion.

There has to be both intensity and volume - near maximum effort - for glucose to be released. In the modern world we can create a similar response with high intensity interval training (HIIT) or heavy weightlifting, which would last for prolonged periods of time. Crossfit style workout routines are just like that.

We don't have to train as hard to be fit but there are other health and mental benefits to pushing ourselves through the dirt like that, which are superior to steady state cardio.

All That Work for Nothing?

But isn't this counterproductive? As in, doesn't establishing ketosis take a lot of time and effort which will all be in vain by consuming carbs? That is true and ketosis can be followed as a long term thing which will be very healthy.

However, on the Keto Cycle ketosis *per se* isn't the purpose. By controlling insulin, which is much more important, for the majority of the time, we'll be able to get all of the benefits of ketones without actually entering into the deepest stages.

The initial adaptation period is vital for creating these pathways within us and teaching ourselves to use an additional fuel source.

Moreover, one short occurrence of carbohydrate consumption will not actually kick us completely out of ketosis, if done properly. If the insulin spike is quick and the glucose is absorbed efficiently then our blood sugar levels will be re-established faster and thus we will get back into our fat burning state by the next day. It just needs to be done strategically.

To maintain our adaptive pathways, we need to occasionally change things up. This way we'll be able to remain efficient with all types of fuel and not become resistant to any.

The cyclical ketogenic diet (CKD) is the less stressful and more sustainable version of nutritional ketosis. We will not have to worry about the overconsumption of carbohydrates or protein. Instead, we will simply stick to our default low-carb eating for a certain period and then incorporate refeeds according to our needs. This way we will not have to chase ghosts and mMol-s by pricking our fingers with needles or be afraid of consuming too many vegetables.

Keto Adaptation vs Nutritional Ketosis

There is a difference between keto adaptation and being in nutritional ketosis. The latter is the actual metabolic state with the appropriate levels of blood sugar and ketone bodies during which we're utilizing fat as the primary fuel source. The former is the pattern which we've gone through and have created these pathways within us. It means that our body knows how to do it without being on it at every specific moment. Using fat to produce energy isn't foreign and the body can thrive despite the presence of glucose.

Keto Adaptation	**Nutritional Ketosis**
Fat burning machine	Extreme fat burning
Ketone production	Altered metabolism
Fat utilization	+0,5 mMol blood ketones
No need for glucose	Fat as primary fuel

On this program, we're not fully keto adapted but at the same time we are because of our ability to function effectively. The degree to which it happens depends on how deep of a state we're in.

The strategical refeeds should be structured and planned carefully. To not get too far away from our adaptation we have to be as careful and selective as before.

In the perfect scenario we would be in ketosis for several days and then, followed by an intense workout session, consume a high amount of carbohydrates that would replenish our muscle glycogen stores and let insulin instigate other metabolic processes. This way normal blood sugar levels will be re-established quicker and the body can return to its fat burning state. It will kick us out of ketosis, but only for a short amount of time. Getting back in requires some adaptation again but if the refeed is done correctly then it can even happen by the next morning.

To prevent any other forms of metabolic alteration from taking place the surge of insulin has to get in, do the work and get out. We need to bust the door open with our guns blazing, make the kill and jet out of there, leaving no signs behind.

These strategical refeeds include high amounts of carbohydrates but we shouldn't forget about other macronutrients as well. Protein is still necessary for maximum recovery and augmentation, as is fat. However, we won't be suffering any consequences for our health or performance if we neglect them for a day. Moreover, at those times we should actually avoid fats because of potential glycation. To maximize our results and not damage our wellbeing we ought to consume them separately from one another.

That short occurrence won't jeopardize ketosis or other pursuits. Being an active individual allows us to get away with a lot and doing it strategically will actually benefit us. Unless you have some sort of a medical condition we shouldn't be afraid of the useful effects of insulin and high amounts of carbohydrates.

Chapter IV
The Standard Cyclical Ketogenic Diet

We can use both ketones and carbs to enhance our training. We would be fine following the regular approach, but when you look at the intense training we're going to be doing it's safe to say that we could need all the help we can get.

The cyclical ketogenic diet (CKD) in a nutshell – you eat keto for a given period and then have massive refeeds with a lot of carbohydrates. Bodybuilders in particular use it to deplete their glycogen stores in preparation of a show and *"carb up"* before stepping on stage. This will make their muscles look fuller and more vascular.

The cyclical ketogenic diet has been used by bodybuilders and strength athletes ever since the 20th century. Vince Gironda with his *Steak & Eggs Diet* comes first to mind. He would prescribe eating close to zero carbs for 5 days and then eat carbs on the 6th. This by default put him into ketosis and helped him to burn insane amounts of fat while still filling out his muscles every week.

In 1995 Dr. Mauro DiPasquale published a book called *The Anabolic Diet* which basically followed the same protocol but with less restrictions. You got to eat all keto-friendly foods with no constraints, other than the macronutrient percentages.

During the week, the macros would be roughly 55-60% fat, 30-35% protein and no more than 30 grams of carbohydrates (<5%). After 5 days you'll have suppressed insulin so much that your body will be solely burning fat.

Then, come Sunday, you perform a big turnaround[xxii]. You would go through a 36-48 hour period of carbohydrate loading, by hitting the carbs HARD. Pizza and beer are okay, and the macro guidelines are 30-40% fat, 10-15% protein and 45-60% carbohydrates.

By limiting the carbs during the week your insulin levels will drop and glucagon levels soar significantly. Once you start stuffing your face with glucose again, insulin will rise dramatically.

In response to this exaggerated carb load, your body will firstly shuttle that sugar into muscle glycogen, which also increases the overall levels of your glycogen stores more than a high carb diet would. Amino acids are driven into the cell and an even greater anabolic response occurs. You'll also experience higher levels of relaxation because of carbs releasing more serotonin.

After the refeed, your body will be buzzing with glucose. Your muscles will be full of glycogen and extremely vascular. If you're already at quite a low amount of body fat, then your veins will be popping out like crazy. When you go to the gym the next day, you'll be getting one the best pumps of your life.

For aesthetic and purely hypertrophic purposes, the CKD is a very good option. It enables you to get the fat burning effects of ketosis, while still getting the augmenting advantages of carbohydrates and the increased water retention they cause.

John Kiefer has similar approaches with his *CarbNite Solution* and *Carb Backloading* programs.

- *CarbNite* follows the same pattern of eating ketogenic during the week and then having a massive carb load. The only exception is that the refeed will last only for half a day – starting after 3-4 PM and lasting until bedtime.

- *Carb Backloading* incorporates carb rich meals strategically several times throughout the week. On your harder training days, say for instance heavy squats and deadlifts, you have a big dinner after 7 PM with vast amounts of high glycemic carbohydrates that would shuttle the nutrients into your muscles. The frequency would depend on the intensity and the goals of the individual. If the purpose is to put on as much body mass as possible, then it can be done almost every other day.

These strategically conducted CKD refeeds can happen in several ways. You can either do them only in preparation of an event, once or twice a month, every week, or even more frequently, after 3-4 days. It all comes down to how you choose to structure your routine and what are your goals. Test and experiment.

Despite of the high amount of carbs, you won't be jeopardizing ketosis as much as you'd think. If you're training hard, then you're already very insulin sensitive and your muscles will happily use that glucose to replenish glycogen.

Chances are, you'll be in back in your fat burning state the following morning, at least within a few days.

During the first 2 days, Monday and Tuesday, your system will be running on both all that extra glycogen and free fatty acids derived from your keto foods. Wednesday until Friday your glycogen stores will be limited again and you'll be burning fat exclusively.

The standard CKD involves 1-2 days of refeeding after exhaustive exercise. On the first day you eat only high glycemic carbohydrates and on the second you eat low glycemic ones. This overcomes the limiting time-factor of glycogen resynthesis.

However, in my own experience, I don't see any significant benefit to this. If you're a natural athlete, then you don't need to lengthen your refeed any more than one day, one massive meal, really. This will benefit your health and keto adaptation that much more.

That's why I'm advocating an approach similar to that of *CarbNite*. You eat ketogenic throughout the week and then, on one afternoon in the weekend, you begin to feast on some carbohydrates until bedtime. It's more sustainable this way and, unless you have a competitive reason or an upcoming athletic event, you don't need to carb load for several days.

That's why the Keto Cycle is different from that and includes only one day of eating carbohydrates.

On your refeed days, you can basically get away with almost anything. In my own experience, I've managed to eat approximately 1000 grams of carbs and still lose fat by the morning. Most of it will be shuttled into your empty glycogen stores at an instant, making it seem like all of the sugar disappeared into a black hole. You can even eat pastries, candy or whatever.

On the CKD, your body will go through dramatic changes every week. First, you'll be eating close to zero carbs and then you'll be stuffing them down your throat in immense quantities. That's why it's important to know when to stop your refeed.

Chances are, you'll have an unlimited appetite, as simple carbohydrates and sugar can become an addictive drug once you start eating them with no limits. It probably isn't a problem for anyone of us hard pushing athletes to consume more than 5000 calories in one day. You don't want to be putting on any excess body fat.

When you start to feel puffy or bloated you should stop your refeed. If you're an experienced bodybuilder or someone who is used to quantifying their food intake, then you should easily tell when you've had enough. It may also be that this small bloat is only an initial response. When it happens, move around a bit or wait an hour or two. If it passes away, then you can continue eating more carbs.

This will vary between individuals and depends on a lot of things, such as the amount of lean body mass, body fat percentage, insulin sensitivity, glycogen depletion, the amount of training done that day and at what intensity. You can't possibly predict exactly when you've hit a point of diminishing returns. Just trial and error.

If you're preparing for a physique competition, then you'll greatly benefit your body composition by following CKD. About 2 weeks prior to the show you'll go through a phase of eating less than 30 grams of carbs and start limiting your water intake, which will deplete your glycogen stores completely.

Then, 2-3 days before stepping on stage you start to slowly incorporate carbs back in. You're not going to be having massive cheat meals because you'll get bloated. Instead, you eat high amounts of carbohydrates to increase vascularity and make your muscles full of water again.

At the day of the event, eat simple carbs to make your veins pop out even more. Drink distilled water, increase potassium intake and calcium, and reduce sodium 24-hours before the contest. Once you step on that stage, you'll be looking at your best.

The Downside to the Standard Cyclical Ketogenic Diet

However, one recent study (Wilson and Lowery *et al* : 2015) comparedcyclic ketogenic dieting to normal ketogenic dieting [xxiii]. They calorically restricted subjects by 500 calories a day, and the cyclic subjects had a normal carbohydrate diet on

Saturday and Sunday. All participants did high intensity and resistance training.

Both groups lost 3 kilograms of body weight—but there was a really big catch. The SKD group lost nearly all fat, while the individuals on CKD lost 2 kilograms of lean mass. What caused this? The traditional keto group was in ketosis the entire week, whereas the cyclers didn't establish ketosis until Thursday. Thus, they were only in very mild ketosis twice a week. Additionally, while SKD went up in strength and strength endurance, the CKD group declined.

Although this study might indicate that long term keto-adaptation might be superior to cycling with carbs, I would still take it with a grain of salt. (1) The refeeds might have been too small for any enhanced anabolic effects to be induced, (2) having 2 days of refeeds may affect ketosis more negatively than one big carb loaded dinner.

The reason is that your body doesn't really want to cause random metabolic changes. Like eating one ketogenic meal won't put you into ketosis, you won't really get kicked out of it by having a carb hefty one either. After prolonged periods of keto-adaptation (1-2 months), your liver enzymes will be completely altered into preferring fat for fuel. Bringing glucose back in for one evening won't immediately change that. However, if you do it several days in a row, your body will happily revert back to a sugar burning metabolism and make you climb that mountain again.

That's why I would imagine that the Keto Cycle with one day of refeeding is better than the commonly used CKD version where you eat high carb for 2 days straight. I've used both of them and I must say that the Keto Cycle is better for ketosis as well as performance.

Chapter V
Who Should do the Cyclical Ketogenic Diet

Surprise! Surprise! Both carbs and fat aren't bad for us. It's just that people tend to eat the wrong things, in wrong amounts and at the wrong time. Of course whole foods are a lot healthier and quality matters first and foremost. It's just that the actual context of the situation is much more relevant.

Before you jump in head first, you should also consider your own conditions. The cyclical ketogenic diet is not for everyone and it has to be done correctly for it to work.

You have to first ask yourself some questions.

- **What am I trying to accomplish?**
    - If you're goal is pure weight loss, then you can either stick to SKD or have longer keto cycles.
    - In the case of performance and muscle building, you would benefit from more frequent refeeds.
- **How long have I done keto?** Of course, the first condition is to get into nutritional ketosis. Otherwise you won't be able to create these fat burning pathways

within you. Initially, you should follow SKD for about a month, before you try CKD. It can be done with 2-3 weeks as well, but the longer you do it the better you become at using ketones for fuel.

- **What's my medical condition?** If you're diabetic, then it would be better to stick to strict nutritional ketosis. Eating some clean carbs won't damage your health on the Keto Cycle but if you want to reverse your illness completely, then I would stay on SKD.

- **Do I need carbs?** Some people react better to keto than others. It mainly has to do with how well adapted you are. Being psychologically dependent of carbohydrates may also create a placebo-like feeling of exhaustion. Your body is fine, but your mind is still addicted to sugar. One thing for sure, the longer you stay in ketosis the better you become at burning fat. At first your performance may suffer but after a while you can even build muscle on a low carb diet, like I have.

We already answered the overarching question: Do you need carbs in the first place?

Not for survival, as it's the only macronutrient we don't need. The brain needs about 30 grams a day, but that can be created by the liver through gluconeogenesis.

Not for muscle glycogen synthesis either. Glycerol and amino acids get the job done as well. What's more, muscle glycogen gets resynthesized with time as well. Even amongst endurance athletes, glycogen gets refilled almost completely within the first 24 hours.The only benefit to eating easily absorbable carbohydrates would be that they get the job done faster.

Nevertheless, following the Keto Cycle is still very beneficial. If you want to maximize your physical performance, stay ketogenic and eat carbs at the same time, then this approach is perfect for you.

The problem with most low carb diets is that they don't solve the energy crisis very efficiently. If you don't give your body a substitute for glucose, then you'll stay into the peripheral zone which is the worst place to be in, if you're training hard.

That's why a lot of people experience bonking on diets like Paleo. You can't expect to see great results in terms of strength and muscle gains this way. If you're working out hard, then you need either ketones or glucose. The Keto Cycle will give you both.

How to Workout on Keto

Our approach would have to depend on our level of adaptation. At first, the body is still quite glucose dominant and prefers the glycolytic pathway. To do that, it will either cause sugar cravings or cause muscle catabolism during exercise.

Every time you have excess glucose circulating your blood stream, you're impeding keto adaptation. As glucose goes up, ketones go down, because they're conflicting fuel sources.

That's why it's best to stay aerobic, at least during the initial phase. You won't be able to perform on high intensities anyway.

A good rule of thumb is that when you're breathing hard, you're being more anaerobic. IF you're able to breathe easily through your nose, then you're aerobic.

You should lay your ego aside for the time being and stick to lower intensities. This period is a great opportunity to focus more on endurance, mobility and less on resistance training. Keto weight training is possible even during adaptation. To teach your body how to use fat for fuel faster, you'll have to be mainly aerobic. At least for the majority of the time.

Once you've gone through about 2-3 weeks of eating low carb, you'll probably be in ketosis. Your body will have gone through the alteration of its own biology.

Now, you've adapted to using fat and ketones for fuel. The longer you continue, the more effective you'll become. Your energy levels will improve and so does your training. You'll see what it's like to workout on keto and it feels quite good.

If you experienced an initial drop in performance. It happened because you underwent a small energy crisis which you have now overcome.

During aerobic exercise you're using solely ketones for fuel. This will also transition over to the anaerobic system. You'll be able to perform at 90% of your maximum equally as good as on glucose.

Your muscle glycogen stores get replenished despite the non-existing presence of lots of carbohydrates. Because of your ability to use your own body fat for fuel extremely efficiently, you won't tap into them that often either. When you do, they can be restored after some time even on a ketogenic diet.

If you're working out at high intensities almost every day, then your body won't have enough time to replenish its muscle glycogen. That's where the carb refeeds come into play and will give you enough fuel to maintain your performance.

Chapter VI
Enter the Keto Cycle

Now that we know everything we need to know about ketosis and carb refeeds we can enter the Keto Cycle. I'm going to give you a step-by-step guide how to put it into action and automatic motion. It's a 3 stage process that then begins to recreate itself.

At first you have to do everything according to plan, because you need to go through certain stages of development and adaptation. Afterwards you can begin to adjust the cycle to your own needs and circumstances.

There is nothing written in here that hasn't been researched, tested, quantified, retested and optimized for countless times by yours truly.

Usually the cyclical ketogenic diet is used by low carb athletes to top off their body's glucose reserve the day before a competitive event. Also by physique athletes, like bodybuilders, to "carb up" before stepping on stage to make their muscles look more full and vascular. This is accompanied by 1-2 days of high carb intake.

However, the Keto Cycle doesn't have to be used only for professionals who are competing. It's simply a way for the individual who trains intensely but eats low carb to improve their performance and health at the same time. That's why this approach doesn't include several days of refeeding but only one big carbohydrate rich meal.

Keep in mind that the Keto Cycle is never stagnant and changes with time. This is only a template that will get you started. As the conditions of your body change so should your approach.

Stage I
Adaptation.

First off, we want to get into nutritional ketosis.

This will teach our body to use fat for fuel and show us how it feels like. Moreover, it's necessary to set the stage for the upcoming phases as well.

To achieve this, we need to do one of the two things – fast for a prolonged period of time or start eating a ketogenic diet. We're actually going to do both which will thus increase our speed of adaptation.

Instead of eating breakfast we'll be pushing our first meal later into the day.

After a full night's sleep, we're already in mild ketosis and using our own body fat to a certain extent. Within a few hours, human growth hormone skyrockets and our body goes through a period of autophagy which is actually good for us.

Additionally, cortisol is also elevated and consuming food right away isn't optimal. Rather than stopping all of those processes from taking place we ought to get out of our own way and take advantage of it.

Drink lots of water and if you get hungry make some tea or coffee which will blunt your appetite. Use that time period for being productive and experience mental clarity.

At about noon have a small ketogenic meal, which will actually extend the fast.

Eggs or some fatty meat with spinach, covered in lots of butter, has been my go-to for a long time. The macronutrient ratios are important. To prevent immediate glyconeogenesis we should not go higher than 40 grams of protein and keep carbohydrates below 10 grams (without the fiber). Of course, as much fat as we would like. It tastes amazing and will satiate us for a long time. Drinking a warm glass of lemon water is acceptable and advisable as it will produce digestive enzymes.

After that, return to your other daily activities. You shouldn't be hungry at all until dinner time. If you do, then make another dish with the same macronutrient properties.

The more fat you eat the more ketones you'll produce. To increase the speed of adaptation you could also take teaspoons of MCT oil or butter every few hours. However, I don't think that's necessary and we can circumvent that by simply adding more fat to our meals.

In the afternoon we'll be doing some training, which will deplete our glycogen stores.

During the adaptation period we shouldn't expect to make any significant improvements in performance. Instead of training extremely hard we should take it as a time to de-load and focus on mobility to not lose strength.

To release glycogen, we ought to focus on higher volume and time under tension. Calisthenics, yoga and weightlifting are perfect for that. HIIT cardio ought to be completely avoided because of the glycolytic demands they put on the body. Without any carbohydrates to replenish our glycogen stores afterwards we would become too catabolic with our own tissue. The reason is that at this point the body doesn't know how to completely utilize ketones yet.

Between 5-8 PM we'll be having dinner.

The idea is to consume the majority of our calories in the evening. You might think that eating before bed will make you fat but actually the opposite happens.

Nutrient partitioning and protein synthesis gets increased later in the day. It will make us sleep better and is also a great mental exercise. Rather than going through the day constantly eating we're being productive and can then relax in the evening.

The meal should still be ketogenic but can now have more calories. Steak, salmon, pork chops, chicken thighs are excellent sources of fatty protein. Broccoli, cauliflower and kale are very fibrous and taste amazing once coated with butter and olive oil. Additionally, some avocados or nuts add variation.

For most optimal cognitive benefits eat eggs and oily fish, such as sardines, mackerel, trout, anchovies and sprats. Of course, stick to organic, grass-fed and free-range as much as possible.

This is what a day of eating would look like during the initial phase. Fasting through the morning hours is important as it sets the stage for the evening. Snacking on additional fat to produce extra ketones would be beneficial but not entirely necessary as eating tablespoons of pure butter is still a habit we don't want to have despite the utility.

The length of the adaptation period varies and it doesn't actually matter that much. Unless you want to achieve strict nutritional ketosis as a long term thing then follow this for 2-3 weeks and move onto the next step

Stage II

Replenish and Supercompensate.

The initial adaptation period might be quite difficult. If you're used to eating a lot of carbohydrates, then your body will show signs of withdrawal. However, if you stick to it and have patience it will get enjoyable.

At some point you just start to feel great and full of energy. Your physical as well as mental performance improves and you're on top of the world. Whether you're in full ketosis or not it doesn't matter. The purpose is to simply create these pathways within us and learn how to use fat for fuel.

Now that we've made some progress it's time to shake things up a bit.

By the end of those 2 weeks you'll probably see some changes. Your mind has been sharp and fresh all of the time but your body has been completely flushed from carbohydrates and looks flat or drained. This is only loss of water weight.

To reignite some of the other metabolic hormones within us and to start building upon this foundation we need to bring back some glucose. It might feel like doing so isn't necessary as you've just started to get used to ketosis. However, in the long run it will benefit us and won't actually hinder our adaptation that much. We just need to go through it several times and then make our own adjustments.

After those 2 weeks pick a day on which you're going to have carbohydrates. This requires a lot of meticulousness and as much caution as during keto. To get the most bang for our buck we still need to follow some principles. There is a lot of things that could go wrong here which would undermine all of our efforts.

On that special day fast for longer than you normally would. Instead of having a ketogenic breakfast simply have coffee and prepare to work out later in the afternoon. The reason is to not have any large amounts of fatty acids circulating the blood stream once we're going to raise insulin. Additionally, working out fasted will release that much more growth hormone and make the muscles absorb glucose more efficiently.

Heavy resistance training is best suited for that day. Because we're in very deep ketosis we won't feel any different and can still exercise quite hard. In my own experience, I'm usually able to hit personal records while having not eaten anything for 24 hours. At the moment it has become a weekly thing for me and it feels extremely empowering afterwards. We simply need to focus and not make a big deal out of it. That's where our other mental faculties get cultivated as well. However, you don't want to take it too far as you're still being catabolic. Know your limits but still try to exceed them. Train hard but don't push yourself through the dirt like a maniac.

At about 4 or 5 PM the stage is set for ultimate supercompensation and enhancement. We're going to flip the switch from catabolism to anabolism.

Our muscle glycogen stores will be completely drained and yearning for fuel. We've been breaking down tissue the entire day and our body will be buzzing with all of the beneficial hormones. By that time those effects will have settled in and can now augment our being. Growth hormone, testosterone and insulin sensitivity are entering the heights of outer space, not to mention the euphoric feeling of empowerment we've attained. At those moments we will feel invincible and truly Superhuman.

In order to repair the damage done and enhance ourselves even further we need to recover from all of that strenuous stimulus.

Break the fast with something high in carbohydrates for quick absorption. According to optimal nutrition the right things at that time are foods with vast amounts of glucose, such as white rice, potatoes, honey or dark spotted extra ripe bananas. At this point some of the processed food, such as dextrose powder, whey protein and refined carbohydrates, are actually beneficial, as this is the only time we want our insulin to skyrocket and fill our blood stream with glucose. Gluten isn't an issue either, as one contamination with it won't kill us. It's actually not a bad idea to eat just a little bit to not build up any intolerances to grains. However, it may have some cognitive side effects the next day. Therefore, clean foods are most optimal for holistic results.

Don't hold back and consume more calories than you normally would. In order for the supercompensatory effects to kick in we need to go slightly overboard. Think of it as a feast our ancient hunter-gatherer forefathers would've had once they found a beehive.

Add in some lean protein, such as whitefish, chicken breast or cottage cheese for the necessary amino acids. Don't make it an excuse to mindlessly indulge in pizza, burgers or French fries because they also have a lot of fat. Keep fats as low as possible for the spike to be quick and sharp. Basically, eat completely opposite to keto. Do this throughout the evening and don't worry about it.

With insulin now being elevated our muscles will absorb all of those nutrients and boost our metabolism. Thyroid restores functioning and our health actually improves because of that. Like I said earlier, the Superhuman diet takes it a step further beyond that and approaches optimal nutrition objectively.

After not having any carbohydrates for 2 weeks we've become extremely sensitive to its stimulus. In fact, it might get too hard to bare. You'll feel your blood pumping at an increased rate and might even experience slight shaking. After a few hours of eating insulin levels will drop again and you'll feel drowsy which is perfect for having a good night's sleep.

The next morning you'll see several things. You probably gained some water weight because of the carbohydrates. Don't worry, it's only temporary bloating, which will disappear the day after, not actual fat gain. On the other hand, you look more vascular and feel leaner than before. In ketosis you were completely flat but after this surge of insulin you'll have veins popping and your muscles are fuller. What's best about it is that you'll happily return to your ordinary ketogenic way of eating.

At this point you'll definitely not be in nutritional ketosis. However, that's fine as your body will still readily accept fat as a source of energy. Start following the menu of Stage I again and you'll feel great in no time. The process of adaptation will be quicker and not as difficult as before. After a few days you'll get your foot in the door once again. However, getting into ketosis isn't the purpose anymore. What we're doing now is simply controlling insulin and avoiding excessive carbohydrates for other health reasons.

Stage III

The Cycle Begins.

This marks the beginning of the cyclical approach.

In this stage you'll eat keto by default and structure carbohydrate intake only according to your training regimen. Not all of the time do we need to avoid insulin and can actually benefit from it.

In this stage we don't have to be as strict with nutritional ketosis either. Because of having adapted to it previously we don't have to be so meticulous about the numbers and percentages. Moreover, we'll be eating carbohydrates on a regular basis anyway so entering the deepest stages of ketosis isn't our purpose. However, the foods we use should still be ketogenic.

The frequency of which we make these shifts depends a lot on our individuality. How much we train, how hard, how often, other lifestyle factors and preferences have to all be taken into account.

If you're not having that high physical demands, then you might be very well off with following strictly keto. However, if you're training more than an average person then strategically incorporating carbohydrates into the mix will improve your performance while not hindering your cognition or health.

After the first refeed have them once a week and then adjust according to your training frequency and intensity. Sometimes, you'll need to do it more often while at others less.

If you're having these dredging workouts every day, then you would want to replenish your glycogen stores every evening. The key is to simply train in ketosis and use carbohydrates for recovery not as a caloric filler. This way glucose is used for its sole purpose – to provide fuel and replenish muscle glycogen stores. At any other time, fat is a lot better for overall health and cognition. Both of these energy sources are optimal for one end or the other but not together.

The idea is to top off your body with glucose either for muscle glycogen synthesis or in preparation of a competitive event where you could need the extra carbs. Your refeeds can even last for 1-2 days, depending on how active you are.

There are a lot of ways we can structure this. For instance, if you're doing intense resistance training 2-3 times a week then you can get away with ketosis and refeeding once a week. However, if, in addition to that, you also do HIIT cardio, Crossfit metabolic conditioning, Tabata intervals and do Spartan races etc. then you need to eat carbohydrates every other day following those workout sessions. In this case you should be careful with the sources of glucose you use, as having large insulin spikes all of the time can potentially lead to resistance. Low glycemic ones, such as sweet potato, quinoa or buckwheat would be most useful, as they don't have gluten either.

When transitioning over to the cyclical version we should increase our protein intake slightly. Because of not being able to establish full ketosis with 2-4 days we would be better off with compensating the lack of carbohydrates with some additional protein.

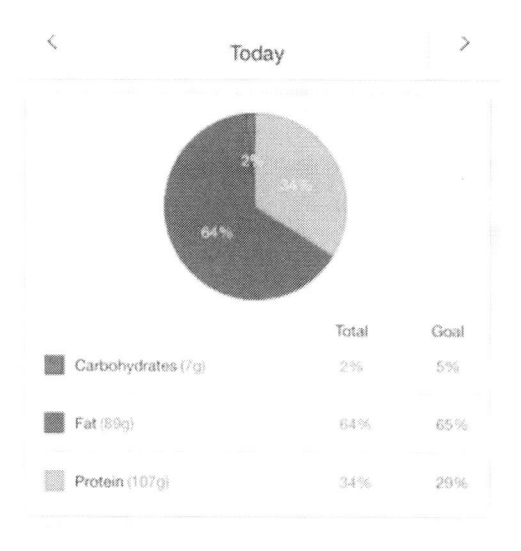

This doesn't mean that we should go over the 1 gram per pound of bodyweight mark as glyconeogenesis still causes excess inflammation. Rather than following the ketogenic macronutrient ratio of 80/5/15 it would be more like 65-70% fat 5% carbs and 25-30% protein. This will increase the circulation of amino acids within the blood stream and maintains performance until the next refeed.

Chapter VII

Mistakes to Avoid

to Not Get Lost in the Eye of the Storm

We know how the Keto Cycle works. It's simple. You fast, eat, train, feast, sleep and repeat. The circle of life.

Because this plan is quite meticulous a lot of things could potentially go wrong. The devil is in the detail and in order to make it work we need to go through all of the possible mistakes we could make. They're the deadly sins we should avoid. Not only would our results suffer but so could our health. In order to not undermine our efforts and wellbeing we have to be very careful.

The most important thing we have to remember is to not consume fat and carbohydrates at the same time. They are contradicting fuel sources and don't work well together. The cause of obesity and diabetes isn't one or the other, it's the combination of both of those.

The standard American diet is high in saturated fat and sugary carbohydrates with low amounts of protein, which is the worst macronutrient ratio imaginable. Ketogenic indigenous people, like the Inuit, were perfectly healthy until they came into contact with white man's white refined food and added it to their traditional way of eating.

Our meals ought to be divided into 2 categories – ketogenic and glycemic, with appropriate macronutrient ratios. Low carb with high fat moderate protein versus high carb low fat moderate protein. We should remember this even when we're not following the plan outlined in this book. It takes so little effort and prevents a lot of damage.

Make a decision about which one you pick and never mix them together. Deep fried French fries are bad for that same reason – the deadly combination of too much salt, sugar and fat. This ought to be kept in mind during our strategic refeeds as well because it will yield lesser results.

Secondly, we should avoid processed food as much as possible. Even though ketosis is healthy it can still be bad for us if we use the wrong types of food. Most of the industrial meat is contaminated with additives that spike our blood sugar. Dextrose, monosodium glutamate and starch are hidden everywhere for that extra taste, which we don't actually consciously experience. Also, sausages tend to have wheat or rice flour in them. To make things easier for you I'm going to add a list of potential hazards we should avoid during our ketogenic cycles. There are probably a lot more but those are the most commonly used.

- The list of ingredients that we don't want to be putting into our mouths: gluten, wheat, monosodium glutamate (MSG), high-fructose corn syrup (HFCS), potassium bromate, sulfur dioxide, food colorings.
- Artificial sweeteners, such as aspartame, cyclamate, xylitol, saccharin, acesulfame-K.
- Transfats, such as hydrogenated vegetable oils, canola oil, rapeseed oil, margarine.
- Preservatives, such as sodium sulfite, sodium nitrate, BHA, BHT, propyl gallate.

We shouldn't become neurotic about this either. When first trying to keto adapt I was very meticulous about tracking all of my numbers. Every gram of carbohydrate needs to be taken into account and will determine the speed at which our body accepts its new fuel source. However, in my experience, that isn't nearly as important as simply controlling insulin and limiting our sugar intake.

Measuring our fasting blood glucose will help us to keep track of our progress and is very useful. If you want the best results as fast as possible, use it but don't be consumed by it. Patience is a virtue for a reason and we might be better off by simply trusting our intuition.

After switching over to the cyclical approach we don't have to be as strict as before. It doesn't matter if we eat 50 grams of carbohydrates or tap into a bit of glyconeogenesis because we're not trying to enter into deep ketosis. We won't be able to make it after a few days anyway. What we simply want is to use fat as fuel for the majority of the week and then refeed ourselves when necessary and appropriate.

There's the danger of going low-carb for too long while still training hard. The consequences might not be immediately visible but it will lead to some hormonal imbalances and thyroid downregulation. If we begin to show signs of too much fatigue, then it might be a good idea to have some carbohydrates. Before doing that, you should also analyze other aspects of your recovery, such as sleep, caloric intake and stress.

Rather than soldiering through and pushing ourselves through the dirt regardless we have to become mindful with our resources. The ketogenic days should be less intense. Attempts of hitting personal records should be structured around refeeds for less metabolic stress.

Another mistake would be to combine too much exercise with excessive fasting. It's great and convenient to eat only dinner but it also imposes some limitations. While in a fasted state autophagy is already making us more catabolic. Adding intense workouts on top of that would do more harm than good. Every once in a while, like in the case of refeed days, it's fine as we will supercompensate, but doing it too often will also cause too much stress.

Also, our training should always be followed by anabolism. After breaking down tissue we need those nutrients and amino acids to repair the damage. Not eating afterwards will make the body cannibalize itself. We don't want our hormonal production to drop. That's why, in my opinion, the 16/8 window is most optimal because we'll get the most benefits from fasting while still being well fed and nourished.

The Deadly Sins NOT to Do

To imprint these lessons into your mind, I'm going to go through all of them once more. Remember them, especially during your refeed days. You're the one who's responsible for your health and well-being.

- DON'T mix high amounts of carbs and fat together. This will make the sugar and fat molecules attach together and causes glycation. Insulin won't have the opportunity to re-settle back to normal, which can lead to resistance or, even worse, diabetes. Eat your carbohydrates with only lean protein.

- DON'T eat too much fruit. When you're having your refeeds, you should focus primarily on glucose rich foods. Not all carbs are the same in terms of their sugar content. Fructose can only be metabolized by the liver and doesn't contribute towards muscle glycogen synthesis. If the liver is already full, then any excess fructose will be stored as body fat. It's okay to have a few servings of your favourite fruit, but keep it low.

- DON'T go overboard with junk food. It's fine to indulge on some garbage every now and then, but for optimal results you would want to eat clean whole foods. The best ones to have are white potatoes, white rice, ripe bananas with dark spots on them (once they go ripe the fructose content in them decreases and glucose increases), honey or some sports drink, like Gatorade.

- DON'T binge. Chances are, you'll be eating a ton of food and carbs. That's okay, insulin will increase that much more and you'll have a greater anabolic response. However, it can be taken too far. I'm not going to lie: you can get away with basically anything. Because your muscles are so empty and you're so insulin sensitive, your body will simply absorb more nutrients than you normally would. Eating about 4000 calories won't lead to any fat gain, as I've experienced. But this doesn't mean you can't be putting on weight. One little cheat meal can potentially reverse all of your week's efforts.

Be mindful of how your body reacts and stop whenever you feel like you've had enough.

- DON'T make it an excuse. The CKD is a great option for those people who want to lose fat with keto and still eat their carbohydrates. It's a great diet because of it brings in variation and leaves room for some cheat meals. However, you shouldn't think of it as a *get out of jail free card*. It's very effective and works extremely well but, just because of that, can be addictive. There's nothing wrong with occasional indulgences, but you should use it as a weapon in your nutritional arsenal to achieve your training goals not as something that allows you to eat limitless junk food.

The importance of not mixing high amounts of fat and carbs cannot be stressed enough. A high fat diet jointly orchestrated will make the insulin response even greater than it would normally be[xxiv]. Because fat slows down digestion, your blood sugar levels will be elevated for a lot longer. The pancreas has to keep pumping out insulin but it won't be able to lower it back down as quickly. What ensues is insulin resistance and potential diabetes.

For muscle growth we need to create an anabolic environment within the body. Training stimulus, protein synthesis, energy surplus and hormones are the variables we need. However, anabolism isn't exclusive to just that. Too much mTOR and IGF-1 will contribute towards the good (muscle growth), the bad (fat gain) and the ugly (tumors).

For longevity purposes we don't want to be anabolic 24/7. Catabolism is necessary for stimulating anabolism but also for keeping the body healthy. The key hormone that dictates the state in which we're at is insulin. That's why our focus should always be in controlling its expression and releasing it only strategically.

The Keto Cycle is a viable and sustainable option for those people who want to build muscle easily and still occasionally eat carbohydrates. For purely aesthetic body composition purposes it's perfect, although it may have slight performance decrements if done incorrectly. You have the blueprint and are well on your way to greatness.

Chapter VIII
Keto Cycle Supplementation

Despite our access to abundant contemporary food we're still missing some key ingredients - the micronutrients. To overcome this flaw there are some supplements we should be taking.

With the industrialization of food all of that has suffered. Our soils are being depleted from their vital life force with the use of fertilizers, spraying of toxic fumes, usage of GMOs, radiation, travel pollution and many other things. All for the purpose of creating more empty calories and food without any actually beneficial content.

On the Keto Cycle there are also some specific supplements we can take to increase our performance and physique even further.

A word of caution. There are a lot of supplements we could be taking. However, that doesn't mean we should start gorging on piles of tablets and numerous pills. It's not about becoming a substance junkie, but a self-empowered being who simply covers all of the necessary micronutrients through the usage of natural yet still manufactured additives.

We don't need to take a whole lot, simply some which everyone needs and especially those that we're individually most deficient of. That's something we have to find out ourselves.

We don't need to fear these pharmaceuticals just because their artificial form. They are just natural ingredients that have been processed and put into a bottle or a powder.

All of the supplements that I have listed here are least processed and free from any additional garbage, such as preservatives, GMO, gluten, starch, sugar etc. They're keto-proof and friendly.

Additionally, we should always try to stick to real whole foods as much as possible. Supplements are just that - supplementation for some of the deficiencies we fail to get from what we actually eat. They're not magical but simply give us the extra edge.

The effects these products have can be derived from natural foods as well. In the form of a pill or a powder they're simply microscopic and packaged nutrition. Taking them will grant us access to optimal health - the utmost level of wellbeing and performance both physical and mental.

In this list are all of the supplements I am personally taking because of their importance, as well as the additional benefits we get. However, I do not advise anyone to take any of them unless they are aware of their medical condition and don't know about the possible side effects or issues that may or may not follow.

Before taking anything we ought to educate ourselves about the topic and consult a professional physician. <u>The responsibility is solely on the individual and I will take none.</u>

Natural Seasoning

To start off I'm going to list the supplements we should be taking, each and every one of us, as they are something that we're definitely all deficient of and also promote Superhuman wellbeing.

Not everything we consume ought to come in the form of a pill. A lot of micronutrients can be found in unprocessed products as well, we simply need to add them to our diet and reap the benefits. They are most natural and completely free from the touch of man. Therefore, they come first and are of utmost value.

- **Turmeric.** One of the best spices we can use is curcumin or turmeric. It has a lot of medicinal properties, such as anti-inflammatory compounds, increase of antioxidants and brain health. Also, it fights and prevents many diseases, such as Arthritis, Alzheimer's and even cancer. In addition to that, it tastes amazing and can be added to everything. I sprinkle it on all foods and run out quite quickly which is why I also buy it in bulk so that it's cheaper. You can also take a capsule.

- **Ginger.** Continuing on with turmeric's brother. It has almost as much health benefits. In addition to that, it lowers blood sugar levels, fights heart disease, treats chronic indigestion, may reduce menstrual pain for women, lowers cholesterol and heals muscle pain. Once again, bulk or capsule.

- **Cinnamon.** These three create the most important natural spices we should be eating on a daily basis. They're incredibly cheap and easy to come by yet have amazing health as well as performance enhancing benefits. Moreover, they all make food taste amazing. Cinnamon falls into the same category as ginger and turmeric - superfoods, because it truly empowers us. In addition to the same medicinal properties it also increases insulin sensitivity, fights neurodegenerative disease and bacterial infections. What's best about it is that it can be added to not only salty foods but on desserts as well. I even add it to my coffee. The best to use is Ceylon or „true" cinnamon.

- **Green tea.** It isn't an actual supplement but is still extremely empowering. In fact, it can be considered to be the healthiest beverage of the world after water. It improves health, brain function, fat oxidation and detoxifies the system. Additionally, lowers blood pressure and prevents all types of disease, including Alzheimer's and cancer. We don't need to take pills with extracts but can get all of the benefits by simply drinking a cup a day. However, to get all of the benefits we need to be consuming about 15-30 cups. Using a capsule would be very efficient.

- **Garlic.** It has a strong taste and smell but is incredibly healthy nonetheless. Chopping garlic cloves forms a compound called allicin, which, once digested, travels all over the body and exerts its potent biological effects. It fights all illness, especially the cold, reduces blood pressure, improves cholesterol levels, contains antioxidants, increases longevity, detoxifies the body from metals, promotes bone health and is delicious. Because of its flavor it makes a great addition to meals. It also comes in capsuled form.

<u>Supplements you HAVE to Take</u>

Moving on with actual supplements. These things we're all deficient of and they also take our performance to the next level, they empower us.

- **Fish/Krill oil.** It's rich in omega-3 fatty acids, which are great for the brain and heart. The counterpart to that is omega-6, which are pro-inflammatory and bad for us. Omega-6 can be found in a lot of processed foods and vegetable oils, which we would want to avoid anyway. For our body to be healthy the omega-3's need to be in balance with the omega-6's. Unfortunately, that balance can be easily tipped off as every amount of omega-6 requires triple the amount of omega-3 to reduce the negative effects. Additionally, fish oil has DHA, which promotes brain functioning, fights inflammation, supports bone health, increases physical performance etc. Naturally, it can be found in fatty fish such as salmon, herring, mackerel and sardines. Fish oil falls into the same category because of its vital importance for superhuman health. It can be used easily as a capsule or liquidized. Taking one teaspoon a day will drastically improve your life. Krill oil might simply be a more potent and bioavailable source. Make sure to use wild caught sources to avoid mercury poisoning.

- **Vitamin D-3.** This is the sunshine vitamin and is one of the most important nutrients. Life exists on Earth because of the Sun. D-3 governs almost every function within us starting from DNA repair and metabolic processes making it a foundation to everything that goes on. It's embedded in nutritious food, given it has received enough exposure to solar light. Vitamin D-3 fights cardiovascular, autoimmune and infective diseases. Of course, the best source would be to get it from the Sun but that is not always possible because of seasonality and location. It can be consumed as oil or a capsule.

- **Magnesium.** Another foundational mineral. It comprises 99% of the body's mineral content and governs almost all of the processes. Magnesium helps to build bones, enables nerves to function and is essential for the production of energy from food. This is especially beneficial for the physically active. Some people who are depressed get headaches because of this deficiency. Because our soils are quite depleted magnesium needs to be supplemented. It can also be used as an oil on your skin for greater absorption in specific areas.

Supplements Empowered

We have covered all of the supplements we should be taking no matter what, the most important and essential ones. Now I'll get down to the empowering ones.

They are not foundational but beneficial nonetheless. With the help of these we can transcend the boundary between healthy and superhuman performance as they will take us to the next level.

- **Creatine Monohydrate.** Creatine is an organic acid produced in the liver that helps to supply energy to cells all over the body, especially muscles. It enhances ATP production and allows for muscle fibers to contract faster, quicker, and makes them overall stronger. That means increased physical performance with explosive and strength based movements and sprinting. However, it doesn't end there. Creatine has been found to improve cognitive functioning, as it's a nootropic as well, improving mental acuity and memory. Naturally, it can be found most in red meat. It's [dirty cheap](#) and easy to consume, as only 5 grams per day will do wonders and doing so won't make a person big nor bulky.

- **Pro- and prebiotics.** Having a well working digestive system is incredibly vital for getting the most nutrients out of our food. Industrialization has done another disservice to us by destroying all of the bacteria in the food we consume, the good and the bad, and replacing them with preservatives. We might be eating but we're not actually deriving a lot of nutrients. In order to have a healthy gut we need to have a well-functioning microbiome. Naturally, food is full of living organisms. Sauerkraut, raw milk, yoghurt, unprocessed meat all have good bacteria in them. With there being no life in our food, we need to create it within us ourselves. [Probiotics](#) are alive microorganisms in a pill that transport these good bacteria into our gut for improved digestion and immune system. Prebiotics are different, they're not alive, but plant fiber that feeds the bacteria. They're indigestible parts of the vegetable that go through our digestive track into our gut where the bacteria then eat them. If you don't like eating a lot of broccoli and spinach, then you should still get a lot of fiber into your diet.

- **Thyroid supplementation.** The thyroid gland is incredibly important for our health because it regulates the functioning of our metabolism. Moreover, because of its location in our throat it also is a connective point between the brain and the rest of the body. This organ is a part of an incredibly complex system which creates this intertwined relationship between the two. With a low functioning thyroid one will have an impeded metabolism, suffer hypothyroidism and many other diseases because of the necessary hormones will not be produced. Promoting thyroid functioning can be done by taking iodine supplementation or eating a lot of sea vegetables. The daily requirements for selenium can be met with eating only 2-3 Brazil nuts.

- **Multivitamin.** There are definitely a lot of vitamins to be covered for our body to not only be healthy but function at its peak. It would be unreasonable to take too many tablets or pills while neglecting the importance of real food. However, taking a multivitamin that has a lot of beneficial minerals all combined into one bottle is very effective and will most definitely be useful.

- **Maca.** Another superfood comes from the Peruvian mountains and is the root of ginseng. It has numerous amounts of vitamins and minerals in it, such as magnesium zinc, copper etc. Also, it promotes hormone functioning for both men and women, as well as increases our energy production just like creatine does. It can either be powdered or made into a tablet.

- **GABA.** Called gamma-aminobutyric acid, it's the main inhibitory neurotransmitter, and regulates the nerve impulses in the human body. Therefore, it is important for both physical and mental performance, as both of them are connected to the nervous system. Also, GABA is to an extent responsible for causing relaxation and calmness, helping to produce BDNF.

- **Chaga mushroom.** Chaga is a mushroom that grows on birch trees. It's extremely beneficial for supporting the immune system, has anti-oxidative and soothing properties, lowers blood pressure and cholesterol. Also, consuming it will promote the health and integrity of the adrenal glands. This powder can be added to teas or other warm beverages. Or you can grind it yourself.

- **MCT oil.** For nutritional ketosis having an additional source of ketone bodies will be beneficial. MCT stands for medium chain triglycerides which are fat molecules that can be digested more rapidly than normal fat ones, which are usually long chain triglycerides. Doing so will enable the brain to have immediate access to abundant energy and a deeper state of ketosis. Basically, it's glucose riding the vessel of ketones. Naturally, it's extracted from coconut oil and is an enhanced liquidized version of it. Additionally, I also eat raw coconut flakes, which have MCTs in them.

- **Collagen protein.** Collagen provides the fastest possible healthy tissue repair, bone renewal and recovery after exercise. It can also boost mental clarity, reduce inflammation, clear your skin, promote joint integrity, reduces aging and builds muscle. Naturally, it's found in tendons and ligaments, that can be consumed by eating meat. As a supplement it can be used as protein powder or as gelatin capsules.

Keto Cycle Supplements

Now I'm going to share with you the ones that can be used specifically on the cyclical ketogenic diet.

- **Branched Chain Amino Acids.** L-Leucine, L-Isoleucine, and L-Valine are grouped together and called BCAAs because of their unique chemical structure. They're essential and have to be derived from diet. Supplementing them will increase performance, muscle recovery and protein synthesis. There is no solid evidence to show any significant benefit to BCAAs. However, they can be very useful to take before fasted workouts to reduce muscle catabolism.

- **Whey protein.** On SKD you would want to avoid protein shakes because they spike your insulin. On CKD you would benefit from having an easily digestible source of protein. Before you break your fast and begin your carb refeed, make a quick shake to get the juices flowing.
- **Dextrose.** It's basically powdered glucose and very high on the glycemic index. You want to avoid it on SKD, but on CKD it's very useful for a post-workout shake with protein. It's dirt cheap. Use it ONLY when doing the Keto Cycle because under other circumstances you're not doing your health a service.

This is the list of supplements we should be taking. It includes the most important ones, the essential, which we should be taking no matter what, as well as the not so vital that simply make us more empowered and give us the extra edge. Nothing replaces good food, but proper and educated supplementation will fix some of the loopholes.

Bonus Chapter

The Keto Cycle Cookbook

As a bonus chapter I wanted to give you some more ideas about what to eat on both SKD as well as CKD.

In the cycle there are going to be periods of mainly low-carb eating with occasional refeeds. What I proposed was that our meals fall into two distinctive categories which are consumed on different days. **They are ketogenic and glycemic.** Separating them is a must for optimal health and best results. Mixing them together will be detrimental.

Therefore, the recipes listed here will follow the same pattern. The first section will cover some delicious foods and strategies to use while trying to keto adapt as well as afterwards. The second part is about what we should use for our high carbohydrate meals.

Because of individual differences I won't be listing exact quantities but simply convey the idea and how to make something. How much grams of this or that depends on your own personal preference and condition.

Prepare your mind and taste buds to be amazed because these meals are truly delicious. With these few recipes you'll never want to eat in any other way ever again. Let's get to it.

Ketogenic Recipes

Let's start off as if we're trying to adapt to nutritional ketosis. Because of intermittent fasting and pushing our first meal later into the day it doesn't mean we won't be having breakfast. It's impossible to not have it as the definition entails feeding and exiting the fasted state. At lunch we're already using ketones to some extent. To take it a step further and promote their production we have to eat accordingly. I'm going to outline here the ultimate breakfast that we could ever have that will give us abundant energy for the rest of the day.

The Ultimate Breakfast

The most classical and satiating meal we could have are eggs and bacon. They have a lot of fat and protein with the right nutritional profile for high end performance. Additionally, we want some fiber and more fat. Even though I would recommend eating eggs for DHA and cholesterol it might not be possible because of allergies. The substitute for that or meat would be oily fish such as sardines, salmon, trout etc. The omega-3 fatty acids and EPA are even more beneficial for our cognition.

- **Ingredients:**
    - 3 Eggs
    - 1 slice of bacon or 1 oz/28g of fish/sausage
    - 1oz/28g of spinach/collard greens/broccoli/cabbage
    - 1 tbsp butter/lard/ghee/coconut oil
    - Optional additives would be cheese or avocado.
    - The spices would be pink Himalayan salt or regular sea salt, black pepper, turmeric, ginger, Cayenne pepper, cinnamon.
- **Preparation:** Either fry your eggs in a lot of butter, poach or boil them. Don't use too much heat as it will damage the nutrients. Throw in the bacon and mix the spinach in the same grease to coat it with fat.

Approximate calories: 450-500 calories (35g protein/40g fat/2g carbs)

To wash it all down with we would also want something to drink. I'm going to share with you my secret recipe that will change your life forever.

Fatty Egg Yolk Coffee

The name of this recipe might be somewhat shocking. Don't worry, you'll change your opinion once you've tasted it. It's not entirely my own idea and I must say kudos to Dave Asprey the Bulletproof executive. However, my own version of it is even better. If you don't drink coffee you can also use tea as a substitute.

- **Ingredients:**

- Coffee/tea

- 1 tbsp of butter/coconut oil/heavy cream/MCT oil

- 1 whole egg

- 1 tsp of raw cacao nibs, coconut flakes, Chaga mushroom, kelp powder and Chia seeds

- 1/4 of an avocado seed, chopped. Yes, the avocado seed is very nutritious. You won't even notice the taste and will love the crunch it brings to your drink.

- 1 tsp of cinnamon, turmeric, black pepper, sea salt and ginger

- **Preparation:**

  - Brew your beverage and let it simmer for a while.

  - Put the egg in your cup and break it down. If it stays in tact it will poach once you add the hot water.

  - Throw in some cacao nibs, coconut flakes, chia seeds, about 5-10 grams each.

  - Chaga mushroom and sea kelp powder, 1/2 teaspoon each because they're quite intense in flavor.

- o Add 1 teaspoon of butter, coconut oil, heavy cream or MCT oil – which one you like most.

- o Chop down the avocado seed into tiny parts with a knife and put them in the cup.

- o Sprinkle in cinnamon, turmeric, ginger, black pepper and sea salt. You can also try out Cayenne pepper for an extra kick.

- o Then mix it vigorously with a spoon or use a blender to create a nice froth on the surface. Using a blender will break the avocado seeds and other ingredients into an amazing mixture. Shaken not stirred, please.

- o Take a sip and be amazed.

Approximate calories: 250 (10g protein/20g fat/2g carbs)

It looks very appealing and has some pools of grease on the surface. Taste it and be amazed as all of your taste buds will fire up. This beverage gives instant and long lasting energy for hours. You won't experience any crash that accompanies drinking coffee either because the fat slows down the release of caffeine. There won't be any quick spike or drop and the brain will function at its best. All of the neurons will light up with joy and be satisfied.

Bone Broth Soup

One of the biggest downsides to eating keto is that some mineral deficiencies might occur. That isn't caused by the lack of variety in the diet but by the low nutritional quality of our soils and vegetables. To circumvent that we would have to take some supplements. However, there is another way. It's even better and a great way to get in touch with our primal side. When a hunter-gatherer caught an animal nothing was wasted. Meat was a precious source of calories and they ate everything that was edible. Instead of trimming off the fat they went for the good stuff. Liver, kidneys, heart, bone marrow, skin with fat on – those are the most nutritious parts. It's only in today's contemporary society where people get disgusted by them. Culture depicts organ meat as putrid and the lean bits as something pure whereas we would be better off by neglecting none. This recipe transcends this dichotomy between the wild and domesticated by incorporating an ancestral practice into our menu.

- **Ingredients:**
  - Bones of a grass-fed and organically raised animal (chicken drumsticks, beef collar, wild boar bones etc.). Healthy animals will have stronger skeletomuscular structure.
  - Onions, garlic.
  - Optionally some organ meats such as: heart, kidneys, liver, chicken gizzards etc.
  - Spices: laurel-leafs, unground pepper and coarse sea salt.
- **Preparation:**
  - Grab a big pot of water and throw in the ingredients. In order to get all of the minerals from the bones they need to be boiled for several hours on low heat. The longer they do the better. Put it on

the stove at the beginning of the day and just let it sit there.
- Add the organ meats only during the last hour of preparation as they would simply turn to pudding.
- After a while the bones will begin to break down. Joints and tendons are the best because they have a lot of connective tissue attached to them. That's what we're after – the ligaments and the marrow inside. Once that happens the water will turn into a pool of fat and grease which tastes amazing.
- Drops of liquid begin to float the surface and give the soup its flavor. It can be used as a basis for other types of cooking or simply drank as a beverage.
- Storing it is easy as it will turn gelatinous after cooling down which can then be re-heated afterwards.

Approximate calories per 1 cup of soup: 110(5g protein/10g fat/0g carbs).

The bone broth soup is a great way to get in all of the essential minerals and nutrients we need from animals. Not only is it tasty and heart-warming but also very good for the gut. It reduces overall inflammation and promotes the strength of our joints because of the marrow.

Meaty Vegetable Roast-Feast

This is one of the best staple dinners we could ever have. It's quick and super easy to make with little to no effort involved. The actual ingredients aren't as important as we can use anything. What matters are only the amounts and the idea.

- **Ingredients:**
    - Some source of fatty meat. Beef, pork chops, chicken wings, thighs etc.
    - Some source of leafy green vegetables. Cabbage, cauliflower, spinach, broccoli, collard greens etc.
    - Some source of extra fat. Butter, lard, ghee, olive oil etc.
    - Spices according to your liking.
- **Preparation:**
    - Grab a pan and add all of the ingredients by placing the greens on the bottom and the meat on top. Sprinkle bits of coarse sea salt on the meat so it would melt into it. Additionally, you can squeeze some lemon juice as well. Pour a bit of water into the bottom. Don't add any extra fat yet.
    - Put it all in the oven and let it cook for about 30-45 minutes. As its starting to be finished throw some butter on top. Don't heat olive oil because it will oxidize and cause inflammation. Use it afterwards as dressing instead.

- Mix all of the vegetables inside the fat. As a sider you can add some avocados or nuts. Dinner is served.

Approximate calories for 1 pound of dish: 750(50g protein/60g fat/6g carbs).

Cauliflower Pizza

The most amazing and versatile food at our disposal on keto is cauliflower. It can be used to substitute almost anything we're used to having: mashed potatoes, rice and pizza. This recipe will teach you how to have your gluten-free-low-carb crust that fits ketosis perfectly.

- **Ingredients:**
    - 1 head of Cauliflower
    - 2-3 Eggs
    - 1 cup of Tomatoes
    - ½ cup of Cheese
    - 1 oz/25g of olives
    - Seasoning and herbs of your choosing.

- **Preparation:**
    - Take the entire head of a cauliflower and cut off the florets.
    - In a food processor shred them all into bits and pieces.
    - Add in an egg or two and blend the mixture.

- Spread the mixture on a pan and put it in the oven for 30 minutes at 375 F/190 C.

- This will turn into a crust and creates texture.

- Add the tomatoes and cheese on top and let it cook for a while until ready.

The same can be done with zucchini as well. Instead of it being pizza they look like boats instead. Simply cut the vegetable in half and add the other ingredients. Cook it in the oven until the cheese starts to melt down and you'll have a quick meal.

Approximate calories for the entire pizza: 900 (50g protein/40g fat/20g carbs).

Approximate calories for ¼ of the pizza: 250(15g protein/10g fat/5g carbs).

Cheesy Tomato Soup

We don't have to drink bone broth by itself but can use it as a basis for other dishes as well. This recipe is perfect for that and tastes amazing. It will heal our gut and bring warmth into our heart.

- **Ingredients:**
    - Chicken bone broth with 2 drumsticks.
    - ½ cups of Cauliflower or broccoli.
    - 2 cups of Tomatoes.
    - 2 tablespoons of Soft cheese.
    - Optional: ¼ cups of coconut milk or heavy cream.
    - Basil leaves.
    - Seasoning according to liking.

- **Preparation:**

  - Put the drumsticks in the hot water and let it simmer for a while. The meat will cook quite easily and the tendons break down faster because of their low density.

  - Chop down the tomatoes and let them be squashed.

  - Steam the vegetables until soft and smash them.

  - Add the seasoning and cheese to the vegetable blend.

  - Pour in coconut milk or heavy cream to make it thicker and consistent.

  - Stir it all up on a saucepan and let the cheese melt down.

  - Pour together the broth with the mixture and tomatoes.

  - Add the extra basil leaves and *voila!*

Approximate calories: 450(25g protein/30g fat/10g carbs).

<u>Beef Stroganoff</u>

A simple delicious dish you can use to get in the necessary creatine from red meat.

- **Ingredients**
    - 1 tablespoon of butter
    - 1 medium onion, chopped
    - 2 to 3 garlic cloves, chopped
    - 1 pound of grass-fed ground beef
    - 1 tablespoons of heavy cream
    - Salt and pepper

- 2 cups of spinach or other green vegetable

- **Preparation**
    - Add the butter to a heated cast iron pan over medium to high heat.
    - Once it's melted, add the onions and garlic. Cook until soft, for about 5 minutes.
    - Add the beef and cook until desired doneness.
    - Reduce the heat to low and add the cheese on top, letting it melt gently.
    - Add the cream, seasoning and stir well. Let it sit for a few minutes with the heat turned off.
    - Either cook the spinach inside the same mixture or use it as a bedding for the meat. Both options work and taste great.
    - Enjoy!

Approximate calories: 1200-1400 (100g protein/100g fat/10g carbs)

Keto Spaghetti Squash

Another Italian classic that doesn't require wheat or whole grains.

- **Ingredients**
    - 1 spaghetti squash
    - 2 tablespoons of butter
    - 1/4 cup of heavy cream or coconut milk
    - Salt and pepper
    - ½ cups of grated cheese
    - A pinch of basil
- **Preparation**
    - Preheat the oven to 375 F/180 C
    - Slice the squash in half, lengthwise, and remove the seeds and pulp.
    - Wrap both halves in aluminum foil, place them face-up on a baking sheet and bake for about 30-40 minutes.

- Once done, scoop out the flesh with a fork, which will create these spaghetti like figures.

- Melt the butter over medium heat and add the heavy cream, salt, cheese and basil. Cook for about 10-15 minutes at a light simmer, while stirring every once in a while.
- Add the spaghetti squash, mix and enjoy!

Approximate calories: 400 (8g protein/30g fat/15g carbs)

Coconut Milk Ice Cream

Despite the lack of sugar in the diet it doesn't mean that we can't be having something sweet. To be honest, the umami taste of bacon feels like candy. Maybe it's just me. We can still have ice cream and bake cakes using keto friendly ingredients and they're even better. This recipe is completely dairy free and suitable for everyone.

- **Ingredients:**
    - 2 cups of coconut milk
    - 2 eggs
    - 2 tablespoons of butter and olive oil
    - 1 teaspoon of vanilla extract or Stevia (optional)
    - Nuts according to preference.
    - 1 tablespoon of coconut flakes
    - ½ cups of blueberries

- 1 teaspoon of cinnamon

- **Preparation:**

    - Separate the egg yolks and whites.

    - Whip the whites until they turn soft.

    - Mix vigorously or blend together butter, olive oil, seasoning while simultaneously adding in the yolks. Do it one by one and slowly until a smooth mixture forms.

    - Pour in the coconut milk and slowly add the egg whites.

    - Keep mixing it all together to make it more fluffy.

    - It should begin to become thicker after a while. For texture add more eggs.

    - Throw in the nuts, blueberries, coconut flakes and cinnamon.

- You can put it in the freezer for a few hours for it to turn more solid or eat right away. The perfect dessert for a hot day.

Approximate calories: 500 (20g protein/40g fat/5g carbs).

Keto Pancakes

Everyone's childhood is probably filled with memories about having pancakes on Sunday. They're great but not for our health because of the gluten and high-fat-carb combo. Fortunately, there is another solution – the keto way. By replacing some of the ingredients, we can still enjoy a healthy tasty dessert.

- **Ingredients:**
    - 2-3 eggs
    - 2 cups of coconut milk or heavy cream (has twice the calories)
    - 2 tablespoons of butter or coconut oil
    - 2oz/50g of almond or coconut flour
    - 1 teaspoon of cinnamon
    - 1/3 cup of blueberries and coconut flakes
- **Preparation:**
    - Beat the eggs until soft.
    - Pour in cream and flour according to preference and texture.
    - Mix them together with cinnamon.
    - Heat the pan with butter.
    - Pour in the pancake mixture and cook on both sides.

- While in the pan throw some coconut flakes on top.

- Serve on a plate with blueberries.

This recipe doesn't even have to involve flour. We can get the same results by using only eggs and cream. It won't look like batter but there hardly is any other difference.

Approximate calories for 3 pancakes: 650 (40g protein/50g fat/6g carbs).

Glycemic Recipes

Now that we've adapted to nutritional ketosis by eating tasty high-fat meals it's time for our refeeds. Despite the fact that we could eat eggs, salmon, bacon and vegetables coated in butter for the rest of our life and be completely fine with it having strategic occasional surges of insulin will be beneficial. This section of the book covers the high carbohydrate meals we can have during those moments where we break ketosis for a moment and replenish our muscle glycogen as well as ignite other metabolic processes.

Homemade French Fries

The problem with all junk food is that it's high in salt, sugar and fat which is the deadly combo we should avoid at all costs. In addition to that the ingredients are all refined and processed with absolutely no nutritional value. They're simply empty calories that contribute to nothing else other than the growth of our adipose tissue. Insulin skyrockets and all that fat gets stored for famine. Luckily, as we found out with keto desserts we can still have all those amazing dishes by making small adjustments. French fries are one of them. Instead of deep frying them in highly inflammatory oils we can still have crispy snacks that fit into the macronutrient ratios of our refeed days.

- **Ingredients:**
  - White or sweet potatoes.
  - Seasoning such as turmeric, ginger, basil and rosemary.
  - Salt and pepper.
- **Preparation:**
  - Wash the potatoes and leave their skin on.
  - Cut them into small wedges or chip-sized pieces.
  - Cover a pan evenly with the potatoes and add the seasoning.
  - Put the pan in the oven and cook on high heat for an hour.
  - Take the pan out and flip the potatoes around.
  - Cook the other side for 30 minutes.
  - Once the potatoes turn brown and crisp they're done.

Approximate calories per 1 cup: 200 (5g protein/1g fat/50g carbs)

These fries are great as the main part of a dish. They're completely fat free, as long as you don't add any oils, and high carb which is great for refeeds. As a sider you can cook some lean meats such as whitefish or chicken breast for the necessary protein.

Chicken Curry

Rice is a big part of Asian cuisine and tastes great. It's very cheap and easy to make. Consuming rice by itself is bad for the absorption of nutrients and it will actually flush out some of the minerals within the body. That's why we should always eat it together with something else. We can make a tasty dish with a lot of flavors instead.

- **Ingredients:**
    - 2 cups of white rice for insulin and high amount of carbohydrates.
    - 2 chicken breasts
    - 2-4 egg whites
    - 2-3 tomatoes
    - Vegetable stir fry mix according to liking.
    - 1 tbsp turmeric and ginger.
- **Preparation:**
    - Cook the rice and let it steam.
    - Either oven bake the chicken or quickly fry it on a pan.
    - Throw in the vegetables and tomatoes with the steamed rice.
    - Let the tomatoes become squishy and add the seasoning.
    - Add the egg whites and let them poach.
    - Mix it together with the chicken and *voila!*

Approximate calories for the entire dish: 800 (70g protein/2g fat/120g carbs)

Rice Pudding

As dessert we can also use very simple ingredients that taste amazing if used properly. This one is perfect for ending our refeeds with something sweet and glycemic. It has to be done the night before because it requires freezing.

- **Ingredients:**
    - 1 cup of white rice
    - 1 cup of cottage cheese or quark

- 2-3 egg whites
- 2 extra ripe bananas
- 1 cup of blueberries, strawberries or cherries
- 1 tbsp cinnamon

- **Preparation:**
  - Cook the rice with the egg whites.
  - Mix it with the bananas and berries.
  - Add in cinnamon and the cottage cheese.
  - Mix it all together and put it in the freezer for the entire night.

Approximate calories: 550 (30g protein/5g fat/90g carbs)

Beetroot Potato Salad with Honey

We want some micronutrients in addition to only carbohydrates as well. Beetroot is very healthy for our cardiovascular system and blood pressure. However, because of its high sugar content it's out of the question during our ketogenic periods. While refeeding it's the perfect ingredient for something sweet and healthy at the same time.

- **Ingredients:**
    - 1 medium beetroot
    - 1 cup of white or sweet potatoes
    - 1 red onion
    - 2-4 tbsp of raw honey
    - 2-3 tomatoes
    - Seasoning
- **Preparation:**
    - Cut the beetroot and potatoes into small pieces.
    - Either oven-bake or cook them according to preference.
    - Take a bowl and chop in the onions and tomatoes.
    - Put in the beetroot and potatoes.

- o Add the seasoning.

- o Melt down the honey and pour it on top of the salad.

- o Mix it all together and enjoy!

Approximate calories: 600 (15g protein/2g fat/110g carbs).

Low Glycemic Stew

In the case of having refeeds more than 2 times a week it's preferable to limit huge fluctuations of blood sugar for optimal results. After 5 days of ketosis we would want our insulin to skyrocket and it would be beneficial. However, doing so too often will have negative side effects. That's why for those select few who have a lot of intense workouts it's a great idea to eat something low glycemic yet still high in carbohydrates. This will prevent any resistance from taking place while still improving performance.

- **Ingredients:**
    - 2-4 medium sweet potatoes
    - 2-4 cups of carrots and turnips
    - 1-2 onions
    - 1 cup of buckwheat is great for this
    - 1-2 chicken breast or any other type of lean meat
- **Preparation:**
    - Grab a big pot and cook all of the vegetables in it.
    - Cook the buckwheat and meat separately.
    - Once the vegetables are all soft pour out the water.
    - Mix all of the ingredients together and enjoy!

That's it! There's definitely a lot more recipes for both of these cookbooks. These are only a few examples you can use to start off with. It's also an opportunity to get creative and go on another journey of nutrition. Eating healthy is incredibly simple and easy once we know the principles to it. By mindfully replacing some of the ingredients we can have tasty meals and avoid any consequences that everyone seems to be struggling with. On this plan we can have it all because of the knowledge we've attained.

Conclusion

Break the Cycle and Go Beyond

You've almost mastered low carb eating. Now all you have to do is implement the plan and enter the Keto Cycle. It's a constant process of staying in motion with our training and nutrition.

The cyclical ketogenic diet is perfect for the individual who is more than a weekend warrior. It includes both periods of keto adaptation and strategic refeeds that will make you ULTRA efficient at burning fat and glucose for fuel. This makes you stronger, leaner, faster and healthier in general.

You won't have to give up on any food group to reach your performance goals. The Keto Cycle enables you to eat almost anything, but only under certain conditions. At the same time, the healthy meals in this book are so delicious that you don't even have any desire for junk.

I'm also going to share with you <u>a concept of mine called optimal nutrition</u>. It can be grasped under a single sentence, which goes as follows:

Optimal nutrition is eating the right things, in the right amounts at the right time.

I do not know about you but I think there cannot be made a better definition than that. It covers all of what we need to know OBJECTIVELY, meaning that it is not taken out of context and can be applied to any situation. We simply need to decipher it and make it fit our demands.

Keto is a part of that, but it may not fit into the paradigm of optimal nutrition all of the time. For the most part it does. Even myself who trains quite hard feels this way. My body is very insulin sensitive but I still prefer to use fat for fuel.

Optimal nutrition goes beyond CKD and breaks the cycle.

On this note I'm going to end the book.

Stay Empowered

Siim

KETO CARB CYCLE Meal Plan

I've also created a 30 day cyclical ketogenic diet meal plan called KETO CARB CYCLE, which will put ultimately into ketosis and the cycle. It includes 50+ recipes and a meal plan with exact quantities of what to eat, in what amounts and at what time. Check it out.

Get the Keto Carb Cycle at http://www.siimland.com/keto-carb-cycle-meal-plan/

More Books from the Author

Find out how to workout on keto and build muscle from the book Keto Bodybuilding

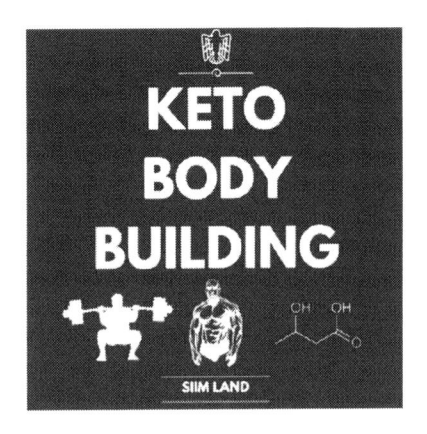

Keto Bodybuilding: Build Lean Muscle and Burn Fat at the Same Time by Eating a Low Carb Ketogenic Bodybuilding Diet and Get the Physique of a Greek God

Simple Keto the Easiest Ketogenic Diet Book

Target Keto the Targeted Ketogenic Diet Book

Vegan Keto: the Vegan Ketogenic Diet

Optimal Nutrition Program: Eat to Become Superhuman

Intermittent Fasting and Feasting: Use Strategic Periods of Undereating and Overfeeding to Unleash the Most Powerful Anabolic Hormones of Your Body

Becoming a Self Empowered Being

Leave a Review on Amazon!

If you liked this book, then I would appreciate it, if you could leave a 5-star review on Amazon. It helps me out a ton and is the least you can do to help other people start a ketogenic diet as well.

About the Author.

Hello, my name is Siim Land and I'm a holistic health practitioner, a fitness expert, an author and a self-empowered being. Ever since my childhood I've been engaged with personal development and self-actualization. As a kid, I made the decision of improving the state of mankind and transcending humanity towards the better. My journey has lead me on an Odyssey of body-mind-spirit, during which I've managed to develop and enhance every aspect of my being. My philosophy is based around achieving self-mastery and excellence first and foremost. What comes after that is the mission of empowering others to do the same. That's what I've dedicated my life to and am doing daily. To do that, I'm always trying to improve upon my own physiology, psychology and biology. I dream of a better world, in which mankind isn't separated from one another and is working towards reaching their truest potential.

Contact me at my blog: http://siimland.com/contact

Reference

Here are the links to academic journals and scientific studies used in this book. If you're on the paperback version, then you can Google them and get the same results.

---

[i] Body composition and hormonal responses to a carbohydrate-restricted diet.
[ii] A high-fat, ketogenic diet induces a unique metabolic state in mice.
[iii] What is an Essential Nutrient?
[iv] Endocrine Notes on Glucose Metabolism (PDF)
[v] Glycerol gluconeogenesis in fasting humans.
[vi] Low-carbohydrate nutrition and metabolism
[vii] The Expensive-Tissue Hypothesis: The Brain and the Digestive System in Human and Primate Evolution
[viii] The Effects of a Ketogenic Diet on Exercise Metabolism and Physical Performance in Off-Road Cyclists
[ix] Nonenzymatic glucosylation and glucose-dependent cross-linking of protein.
[x] The AGE-receptor in the pathogenesis of diabetic complications.
[xi] Advanced glycation end products Key Players in Skin Aging?
[xii] The effects of a low-carbohydrate ketogenic diet and a low-fat diet on mood, hunger, and other self-reported symptoms.
[xiii] The National Cholesterol Education Program Diet vs a Diet Lower in Carbohydrates and Higher in Protein and Monounsaturated Fat
[xiv] HDL-subpopulation patterns in response to reductions in dietary total and saturated fat intakes in healthy subjects
[xv] Short-term effects of severe dietary carbohydrate-restriction advice in Type 2 diabetes--a randomized controlled trial.
[xvi] A low-carbohydrate, ketogenic diet to treat type 2 diabetes
[xvii] Metabolic syndrome and low-carbohydrate ketogenic diets in the medical school biochemistry curriculum
[xviii] Metabolic characteristics of keto-adapted ultra-endurance runners
[xix] Ketogenic diet does not affect strength performance in elite artistic gymnasts
[xx] Grimm O. Addicted to food. Scientific American Mind 2007; 18(2):36-39
[xxi] Low-carbohydrate nutrition and metabolism
[xxii] DiPasquale, M. (1995) *The Anabolic Diet*, Optimum Training Systems

[xxiii] Sharp, M.S., Lowery, R.P., Shields, K.A., Hollmer, C.A., Lane, J.R., Partl, J.M., ... & Wilson, J.M. (2015). The 8 Week Effects of Very Low Carbohydrate Dieting vs Very Low Carbohydrate Dieting with Refeed on Body Composition. NSCA National Conference, Orlando, FL.

[xxiv] Modulation of the exercise and retirement effects by dietary fat intake in hamsters.

Printed in Great Britain
by Amazon